America is Hooked on

After a shaky first season, *Cheers* quickly became a modern television classic—with millions of devoted fans tuning in to the multi-award-winning series every Thursday night without fail. Can you remember the first season? The first show? This warm and wonderful *Cheers* companion whisks you back to the beginning and brings you right up to date—taking you on a glittering tour of the sensational hit TV series in a way you've never seen it before.

BART ANDREWS is the author of countless successful TV books including the definitive *I Love Lucy Book* and *Holy Mackerel! The Amos and Andy Story*.

THE OFFICIAL SCRAPBOOK

BART ANDREWS

with CHERYL BLYTHE

WITH A FOREWORD BY TED DANSON

A SIGNET BOOK

NEW AMERICAN LIBRARY

Published by arrangement with Paramount Pictures Corporation, Inc.

 SIGNET TRADEMARK REG. U.S. PAT. OFF. AND FOREIGN COUNTRIES
REGISTERED TRADEMARK—MARCA REGISTRADA
HECHO EN SECAUCUS, NJ., U.S.A.

SIGNET, SIGNET CLASSIC, MENTOR, ONYX, PLUME,
MERIDIAN and NAL BOOKS are published by NAL PENGUIN INC.,
1633 Broadway, New York, New York 10019

First Printing, May, 1987

1   2   3   4   5   6   7   8   9

PRINTED IN THE UNITED STATES OF AMERICA

*This book is dedicated
with love
to the memory of
Nicholas Colasanto
(1923–1985)*

Acknowledgments

Cheers is a special show, and it took some special people to translate it into a book.

A big thank-you goes to Susan Zilber, director of licensing at Paramount, who made this book a reality when she licensed publishing rights to New American Library editor Jeanne Tiedge, who asked me if I'd be interested in doing a book on *Cheers*.

My undying gratitude to the contingent at Paramount— Amy Rayfiel, John Wentworth, and Jane Klein, who went out of their way to provide facts and photos (and an occasional Xerox copy).

Sean Mahoney, *Cheers* publicist, and Richard Villarino, *Cheers* executive in charge of production, were absolutely invaluable in the preparation of this project, as were their assistants, Britt and Danielle.

Of course, without the sparkling talents of producers Les Charles, Glen Charles, and Jim Burrows and the lead actors who make their creations come alive every week—Ted Danson, Shelley Long, Rhea Perlman, John Ratzenberger, George Wendt, Woody Harrelson, and Kelsey Grammer—there would be no book, and, frankly, no reason to watch TV at 9:00 P.M. Thursday nights.

Thanks to the staff of DeForest Research for nailing down some critical facts, to Rick Beren for his "dry" sense of humor; and to Tom Kershaw of The Bull & Finch in Boston for his time and patience.

A tip of the hat to May Quigley, Ted Danson's assistant, who went out of her way to make things happen.

Thank you, Marc DeLeon, for insisting I watch *Cheers*, not reruns of *I Married Joan* on CBN.

Finally, a word of gratitude to my partner and literary agent, Sherry Robb, for steering me in the right direction; and to Cheryl Blythe for the compass, map, suitcase, provisions, itinerary, passport, and camera—everything it took to complete this literary journey.

Cheers to all of you!

Contents

Foreword

This is a note found scribbled in Ted Danson's 1983 Emmy program:

I'd like to thank the Academy for giving me the opportunity to thank the following people:

Thank you, Glen and Les Charles and Jimmy Burrows, for creating the character of Sam and recreating him week after week. You have taught me to value writers and their work above all else.

Thank you, Shelley, Rhea, George, John, Kelsey, Woody, and Nick. Not only do we do good work together, we have fun doing it.

Thank you, NBC and Paramount, for always providing us with a creative and supportive atmosphere to work in. It makes a difference.

Thank you, Casey, my wife, and all wives and husbands involved in Cheers. *You all are the truly creative ones. Just look at the number of children you have produced over the past five years. We must be doing something right.*

And finally, thank you for watching.

TED DANSON

Introduction

On September 30, 1982, a new situation comedy premiered on NBC. Since it had been placed in a deadly time slot at 9:00 P.M. on Thursday night—with audiences watching the immensely popular *Magnum P.I.* for an hour on CBS at 8:00 P.M. and staying tuned for *Simon and Simon* or sticking with a known entity on ABC at 9:00 P.M., *Too Close For Comfort*—no one seemed to find this unique new series called *Cheers.*

No one, that is, except the critics. Although week after week they lavished the highest praise possible on the producers, the writers, and the cast, the audience just wasn't tuning in and the series seemed destined for cancellation.

Those of us who were lucky enough to catch that premiere episode, entitled "Give Me a Ring Sometime," knew from the moment the main theme song started that *Cheers* was going to be something special. The opening artwork caught our attention and our first look at the gleaming mahogany bar and brass fixtures said someone had put a lot of loving care into this new show.

1

We were captivated by the clever dialogue that spoke of today without trying to be trendy or cute. The show's lead character, Sam Malone, was handsome, humorous, and flawlessly macho. Stranded in this unfamiliar environment, intellectual Diane Chambers touched us with her obvious discomfort and pseudo-bravado. Coach was a delight as he tried to comprehend everything that went on around him, and Carla said all the things we wish we could say and get away with. Norm and Cliff were everyone's Everymen.

We knew this show was just too good to be true, and certainly too good to last. Fortunately, NBC, in the persons of Grant Tinker and Brandon Tartikoff, felt the same way and were determined to see that it did last, even though during its first four weeks on the air, *Cheers* never climbed above number 60 (out of 66 shows) in the Nielsen ratings. Convinced that they had a hit series if only the audience would find it, NBC gave it a full season go-ahead.

When the 1982–83 Emmys were announced, *Cheers* had garnered a staggering thirteen nominations, eventually walking off with five of the top comedy series awards: Best Comedy Series, Best Actress (Shelley Long), Best Writing (Glen Charles and Les Charles), Best Directing (James Burrows), and Best Graphic Design and Title Sequence.

Over the next three seasons, *Cheers* accumulated a total of thirty-six additional Emmy nominations, consistently in the categories of Outstanding Comedy Series, Directing, Writing, Lead Actor and Actress, and Supporting Actor and Actress.

Cheers is that rare breed of show that appeals to the broadest audience—young urban professionals and blue-collar workers alike. Conversation runs the gamut from the Red Sox to Rembrandt, to arguments on the "sweatiest movie ever made." There's something for everyone at Cheers: the witty barbs of Carla, the perpetual confusion of Coach, Sam's womanizing with "bimbos" and his unexplainable determination to have a relationship with Diane, and the daily traumas and triumphs of the regulars.

What follows is a behind-the-scenes look at these very special people and this very special place, Cheers.

A Classic in the Making

Glen Charles, Les Charles, and Jim Burrows have managed that rare feat of creating a make-believe place that we all wish was within walking distance of our homes. For those of us who are lucky enough to have that "corner bar" where we can go anytime we're lonely, or want to share good news, or just hang out with friends, we recognize Cheers' comfortable surroundings and feel like one of the regulars ourselves. And for those of us who don't have such a place, Cheers, the fictional bar of television, becomes that home away from home. We can sit in our living rooms and feel surrounded by friends. Somehow we know if we could walk into that imaginary world, we'd be accepted—no matter what our background, no matter what our story.

All three producers came out of the MTM (Mary Tyler Moore Productions) stable. Brothers Glen and Les Charles started as an advertising copywriter and English teacher, respectively, until 1975, when a sample *M*A*S*H* script on which they collaborated opened television's lucrative doors for them. They went on to write and produce MTM's *Phyllis* and *The Bob Newhart Show* before leaving for Paramount Studios where they wrote and produced *Taxi*. Jim Burrows, the son of legendary playwright/director Abe Burrows, began his directing career with the classic *Mary Tyler Moore Show* and ultimately moved on to direct seventy-five episodes of *Taxi* before teaming up with Glen and Les Charles to create a series of their own.

Perhaps the most challenging job in television is finding a setting for a group of characters and situations that will make people laugh.

Les Charles, the younger brother, remembers, "The very first thing we had in mind was the setting. After working on *Taxi* where the whole concept of the series was a bunch of characters in a place they wanted to get out of [the garage], for a change of pace we wanted to do the opposite—have a setting people *liked* to be in."

Jim Burrows said, "All the quality comedy shows usually work out of one major locale. In those cases, the setting has as much to do with the humor as do the characters."

The first concept for *Cheers* was to set the show in a small hotel—have the main characters be the proprietors and have the stories come from the guests and supporting cast. Glen Charles recalls, "We saw that all the good stories we came up with were coming out of the hotel bar. That opened our eyes. Anyone can walk into a bar voluntarily. Setting a television series in a bar went against the grain, and the challenge began to appeal to us."

This was still a fairly unique idea to television—memorable series include only *Duffy's Tavern* in 1954, *The Corner Bar* in 1972, and the more recent *Archie Bunker's Place* in 1979. The Charles brothers wanted *their* bar to look and feel real, not like the stereotypical bar commonly seen on television. Burrows added, "Bars have been used simply as window dressing, but not really as a setting for presenting honest humor."

Glen concurred: "There hasn't been a bar show that

8

did what was possible—the reality, the conversations. Bars have their own rhythm, their own drama. Almost every human activity takes place in a bar, or is reflected in a bar. The bars on television or in the movies never seem real."

The trio of producers began a major hunt for both a locale and a bar that would appeal to all audiences. They set their sights on Boston, a favorite place of Glen and Mary Ann Charles. Here was a cosmopolitan city that offered a wide range of income brackets, a strong sports-fan appeal, and an ethnically mixed population. It was perfect.

And, it had not been exploited by television. There were only a few other series set in Boston—*Banacek, Beacon Hill, James at 15, Paul Sand in Friends & Lovers,* and *The Young Lawyers*—all short-lived.

The next task was to find a model neighborhood bar. While visiting Boston, Glen and Mary Ann walked across the Common to the exclusive Hampshire House at 84 Beacon Street in the Beacon Hill section of the city. An outside staircase led down to the basement and the Bull & Finch pub.

This was it. The atmosphere was warm and comfortable; the clientele boasted construction workers in hard hats, lawyers, insurance salesmen, policemen, retired people, and college students. Mary Ann pulled out her camera and began taking snapshots of the interior—over seventy pictures in all, showing every nook and cranny, every angle. Here was everything the producers were looking for in a setting, even the exterior staircase, which would allow the feeling of inside and outside without having to build an exterior street set.

With owner Tom Kershaw's permission, the photos were taken back to Hollywood and the massive task of recreating the feeling of the Bull & Finch on Paramount sound stage #25 began. The front entrance is identical

9

to the original, except that the door to the Bull & Finch opens out, and the Cheers door opens in.

Most TV show budgets allow for several different sets, but because *Cheers* would take place almost exclusively in the bar, the entire budget could be used for the one set. The brass is real, the bar stools are covered with red leather, the floor is done in red tile, and the glasses hung over the bar give that touch of sparkle against all the dark wood. With all of this, the show still came in under budget and under schedule. Was this remarkable attention to detail worth it? Richard Sylbert, the art director, and George Gaines, the set decorator, were both nominated for Emmys for Outstanding Art Direction for the finished Cheers set.

The photograph in the opening TV credits is the real Bull & Finch entrance, and the interior staircase going up to the Hampshire House is duplicated as well.

After viewing the first episode, Kershaw remarked, "It was very odd when they gave the upstairs restaurant the name of Melville's. [The producers] didn't know it, but that's my father's name."

Kershaw is both flattered and a little overwhelmed by the popularity of his neighborhood bar since *Cheers* has been on the air. The back room is now called Cheers, waitresses wear *Cheers* T-shirts, and to avoid ashtray stealing, a souvenir stand sits in the entryway selling all sorts of *Cheers* paraphernalia, and a bright yellow *Cheers* flag hangs next to the American flag outside. Eddie Doyle, the manager, recently put up a sign inviting customers behind the bar to have their pictures taken in return for a two-dollar contribution to a children's hospital fund.

The steady tourist trade has scattered some of the old regulars, but Kershaw still claims it's just a neighborhood bar. "*Cheers* fans like to come in and feel the atmosphere they see on television. There's really no other show where you can step into the set the way you can here."

In 1984, the Greater Boston Convention and Visitors Bureau created a "Boston's Brightest Award" to honor those who have done the most to promote the city. The first honors went to the creators of *Cheers;* the governor of the state of Massachusetts got the second award.

There was obvious concern from NBC on the subject of alcohol, a vital aspect of any series set in a bar, but the network's fears were unfounded. "We set out to do a realistic, funny series about a bar that people would want to visit," Jim Burrows explains. "People come into a bar as much for camaraderie as anything else. Some don't even drink booze."

Instead of hiding from the social implications of alcohol consumption, the Charles brothers decided to meet the problem head on and made their main character a recovering alcoholic. "That makes him kind of a heroic figure," said Les Charles.

They did not want to show extensive drunkenness, and stressed to the network the difference between bar humor and drunk humor. "One is falling down and forgetfulness, but the other has to do with conversations that go on, the most trivial and mundane that everyone starts to contribute to. We witnessed a twenty-minute conversation once about canned soups in restaurants, and the bartender was the moderator," said Les.

Cheers is sensitive to the problems of drinking and has gotten its message across very subtly. No character who's had one too many at Cheers is allowed to drive himself home, and the regulars who tip back beers every night ask for a cup of coffee on a cold day if they're still working when they stop by. Cheers is portrayed more as a social outlet than a place to drink.

There was one network snafu the producers had to overcome and that dealt with brand names. In order to preserve the feeling of a real bar, they wanted to stock it with actual bottles. It is a rule of television that you

11

don't show or say names of products. Les Charles said, "It's ridiculous to have someone say, 'Give me a scotch,' or 'Give me a beer.' The names mean a lot in terms of authenticity. That got the network worried about whether we'd be guilty of plugging certain brands. Finally we reached a compromise. We serve a different brand to each customer in the script."

Next came the major task of "peopling" the series. The network was pressuring the creators to use known stars. "We rejected the idea because a show becomes identified in the public's mind as so-and-so's show," Les explains. "We decided to *make* stars instead."

Glen and Les Charles and Jim Burrows read over one thousand actors for the four principal characters:

Sam Malone, Diane Chambers, Coach Ernie Pantusso, and Carla Tortelli. Not only did they need four good comic actors, but the quartet also had to function outstandingly as a team.

Jim recalled, "Each actor read the same scene. Everyone got the same chance. We were looking for actors who could make us laugh by being loyal to the characters. Then we matched them up."

Les added, "We had some surprises. Some actors were terrific by themselves, but not in concert with the others." Glen elaborated, saying, "We tried all kinds of combinations. Casting is vital, especially in this show where there's sexual tension between the two main characters. This hasn't been tried before."

"You can't compensate for wrong casting with writing," Les continued. "It's a killer to try. That's why we spent so much time casting. NBC gave us the luxury of time—six months to put the show together."

The end result was worth the effort. Ted Danson (*Body Heat*) would play Sam Malone, the ex–Red Sox relief pitcher, womanizer, and owner of Cheers; Shelley Long (*Night Shift*) would be the psuedo-intellectual waitress Diane Chambers, torn between logic and lust; Rhea Perlman (off-Broadway and TV movies) was the ideal sharp-tongued Italian tornado, Carla; Nicholas Colasanto (veteran TV director) became the slightly out-of-step ex-coach and current bartender/father figure; and John Ratzenberger and George Wendt would round out the cast as Cliff and Norm, the anchors at the end of the bar.

Jim Burrows said after the first show, "The cast is ensemble. They look like they've been playing together for years. At the core is the relationship between the two people. It's a hot relationship—there's an attraction."

"Romantic comedy is relatively unique in sitcoms," explained Les Charles. "Usually people on a sitcom feel the same about each other on the first show as they do the last. But here, Sam and Diane can end up married and divorced. It can change from week to week."

The comedy of Sam and Diane has been compared to the classic Tracy/Hepburn romantic comedies of the forties. The producers knew they had opened a veritable hornet's nest when they created Sam and Diane. The challenge has been to make sure the characters kept growing and evolving. "Every time there's been a change, we have always felt that we got what we wanted out of the previous stage. If Sam and Diane had married, it would have been boring. If we had come up with any more flirtation between them, it would have been annoying," said Les. Jim Burrows remembers the first season as trying "to see how long we could keep these characters out of bed."

Cheers has broken all the ground rules when it comes to sex on prime-time comedies. Yes, we've seen it in the nighttime soaps, but rarely on a half-hour comedy has sex been so openly talked about: constantly and romantically when Sam and Diane were a "couple"; and sarcastically and bitterly after they broke up.

Back in the fifties when Lucille Ball became pregnant, Lucy Ricardo, after many discussions with the network, was finally allowed to be "expecting," but the word "pregnant" was verboten. In the eighties, *Cheers* has had Carla Tortelli pregnant with not one but two *illegitimate* babies. And they've done it with such finesse, the viewer is not critical over her promiscuity. Carla assumes full responsibility for her actions—a little apologetically at times—and somehow we know that the next time she has sex, there's a strong possibility she'll be right back at Cheers, her growing tummy accentuated, going for those "sympathy tips."

The writing on *Cheers* is very different from that of other sitcoms. "Rather than having someone slip on a

14

A very pregnant Carla with ex-husband Nick Tortelli *(Dan Hedeya)*.

banana peel, we get a laugh quoting John Donne," Burrows explains. "We trust the audience to get the joke. We do not write down. We try to write up." How many other shows made jokes about *Othello* and Anaïs Nin? He admits when they first started, he would call NBC every day to make sure they were okay. "And they called us all the time, too, to reassure us."

"We're playing around with the form a bit," Les

Charles says. "We have stories that come in and out; some don't start until page ten. We're trying to experiment with looser stories, too, and nontraditional dramatic components without a strong beginning, middle, or end format."

Heide Perlman, Rhea's sister and a writer/producer on *Cheers*, agreed, saying, "The tone of the show is intellectual and sophisticated for television. It's concerned with what people deal with in their lives, rather than the cataclysmic events usually shown on television comedies. . . . A sitcom is a 'situation comedy.' It should consist of an everyday situation that people can relate to because it touches their own everyday experiences."

Because of the nature of *Cheers*, the producers admit even *they* don't know where the show is headed from week to week . . . just as in real life, often one word or an event can drastically change the shape of a person's life.

There are people who will take potshots at TV sitcoms, and Les takes it to heart. "People who criticize television don't understand how little time we're given. Usually you just have to settle because of the incredible deadline pressure. Sometimes I'm down on television, too, but other times I'm amazed at how good it is. It isn't better than it is because you have a week to do something that if you had the time, you'd love to spend a year on."

Shelley Long remembers filming the first episode on April 23, 1982. They were still in rehearsal three hours before the audience was due to come in, and there was no ending for the show. Numerous areas for comedy had been tried, and just fell flat. Shelley was already in makeup when she was handed the new scene to be memorized. She explained, "You reach the point, with the audience out there waiting for you, that you just don't care what ending the writers are going to spring on you. You can't worry if someone in the audience is

16

going to say, 'Harold, she just blew her lines. What's wrong with her?' You just go out there and do it."

The ending finally chosen for that first episode had Diane Chambers accepting the fact she'd been jilted by her fiancé and would now be working as a waitress at Cheers. She was giving a long, heartfelt dissertation to an attentive couple about why she was working there when Sam finally interrupted her monologue by hitting a bell. Diane smiled politely, and asked the couple what they would like to order. The man consulted a small book, and then in a heavy foreign accent read: "Where is police? We have lost our luggage."

Jim Burrows tells a story of the first *Mary Tyler Moore Show* he directed, which ended up being one of that series' few so-so episodes. He told Arthur Price, now president of MTM, "On a series of danishes, it's just my luck to get a bagel." Eight years later, when *Cheers* premiered, Price telegramed Burrows, "Finally! You got your danish."

It took almost the entire first season for *Cheers* to build an audience, even though critics weekly lavished praise on this innovative new series. Burrows remembers, "We got calls from everybody telling us what to do with the show. Change the hair, change the wardrobe. Make him weaker, make her stronger. Go for the bigger jokes." The three producers were well acquainted with the viewing habits of the audience, and held their breath hoping people would eventually find *Cheers*, and continued to produce the show their way.

Cheers is currently in its fifth season. The characters have grown up, loved and lost—the same as we viewers have over the last five years. Its success can be placed on brilliant writing that appeals to our intellect one minute and our funny bone the next and an extraordinary cast of actors. Watching, you can almost believe these people come to the bar to work and socialize even on the nights they're not on TV.

17

Starring...

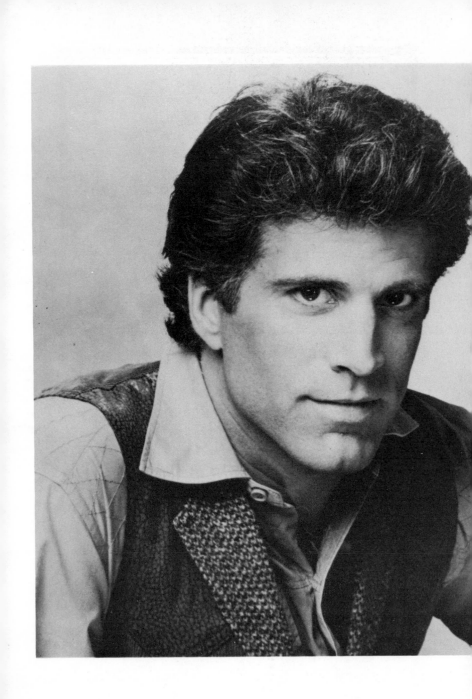

Ted Danson
as
Sam Malone

The womanizing, ex–Red Sox relief pitcher and Cheers owner/bartender is deftly portrayed by Ted Danson. The actor has managed to ride that fine line between making Sam an egocentric, macho, chauvinistic bore and a mischievous little boy. It's hard to get angry with Sam when he's played with such insouciance.

Whereas Sam Malone is terrified of making a serious commitment to a woman, Ted Danson has said, "I was born married." An extremely devoted family man, Ted Danson has become the new sex symbol for the eighties— much to his own surprise.

Edward Bridge Danson III was born on December 29, 1947, in San Diego, California. His family moved to Boulder, and then to Tucson, before settling in Flagstaff, where his father, an archaeologist, became the director of the Museum and Research Center of Northern Arizona.

Ted remembers Flagstaff as "a great place to grow up. Beautiful mountains, deep canyons, horses to ride . . ." His friends were the local Hopi and Navajo Indians, and since there was no television, weekends were spent at the movies. "I can remember going to the movies with my friends and getting confused about whether I should cheer for the cowboys or the Indians. I think we were all just embarrassed."

At age thirteen, Ted enrolled in the Kent Prep School in Connecticut. "I gave new meaning to 'the awkward years.' I was six feet and 120 pounds. I was unbearably skinny with bizarre teeth that I had capped when I was twenty. People didn't know if they should beat me up or laugh."

From Kent, he entered Stanford University and began the dating ritual. Shy and still uncomfortable about his physique, he was constantly worried about rejection. There was one young lady he was attracted to, and knowing no other way to get her attention, he followed her to an acting audition. It was for a Bertolt Brecht play, *Man Is Man*, and he wound up with a small part. Ted Danson had discovered acting.

He transferred to Carnegie Tech (now Carnegie-Mellon University) in Pittsburgh to learn his craft. While there, he met a young actress, Randy, and at age twenty-two, Ted married her. The marriage lasted only five years and the breakup was very amicable. Ted explained that they were just too young, but it did teach him something about himself. "I work better married. I like 'team.' I think you can get a lot done in life as a couple. The support is real powerful."

In 1972, Ted moved to New York, and got his first acting job as an understudy in the off-Broadway play *The Real Inspector Hound*. He graduated to a speaking role and, after a year and a half, left to do the play *Status Quo Vadis*, which opened and closed in one night.

He tried to get work as a male model, couldn't, and signed up with a commercial agent. In between doing performances of Shakespeare in the Park, Ted could be found playing such demanding roles as that of a box of Lemon Chiffon Pie Mix. Dressed in yellow tights and a

box, Ted marched down a New Jersey street, flanked by other actors playing chocolate, butterscotch, and vanilla mixes.

From commercials and Shakespeare, he moved into daytime soaps, where he had a recurring role on *The Doctors*. For two years, he was a regular on *Somerset* and recalled, "I don't think any experience ever scared me so much, plus I was bad at it. I was supposed to be this slimy character who was always trying to put the make on women, but I was quivering so much that the actresses playing the supposedly nervous women were busy trying to calm me down. I had already decided to leave when the show folded."

Single, lonely, and longing for a relationship, Ted tried dating again but wasn't very successful—that is, until he met Casey Coates. She once said, "I thought either he's the sweetest guy in the world or a complete nerd. . . ."

Ted says for him it was love at first sight. "I asked her out to dinner and we talked until four in the morning. It was almost as if she was saying. 'This is what I want in my life,' and I was saying, 'Mm-hmmm. That's good, that's good.' From that night on we were constant companions." Ted and Casey were married six months after that fateful dinner.

In 1978, Ted and Casey moved to Los Angeles. He landed his first acting job in Hollywood in a nonspeaking role on *Quincy* where he played a doctor in an operating room and had a mask covering his face.

Seemingly out of nowhere, Ted Danson was cast as the gentle, unfortunate police officer Ian Campbell, in *The Onion Field*. Although critics and industry people alike were impressed with his performance, Ted said, "It was my first big break, but when I saw the movie I was crushed. I thought I was terrible, that I'd never work again. A year later I watched a second time and realized I was okay. To this day, I still react badly when I see something for the first time."

24

Ted continued to work in television, guesting on such hit series as *Laverne and Shirley*, *Family*, and *Magnum P.I.* He had just been cast in a major role in the TV movie *The Womens' Room*, when his life fell apart.

Casey was pregnant with their first child, and on Christmas Eve 1979, while she was giving birth with Ted at her side, Casey suffered a massive stroke. "In the midst of seeing a baby born, you're so awestruck in the first place, then to have that happening. It was just horrendous."

Fortunately, little Kate was born healthy, but the doctors told Ted that Casey would be paralyzed on her left side. Ted remembers the rage he felt toward the doctors. "Years ago they thought that whatever return of motion you had after ninety days, that's what you'd live with. They've discovered that that's not true. How sad to put a limit on someone and they believe it and it becomes their limit."

Ted wasn't about to let himself or Casey settle for anything less than one hundred percent recovery. One of her nurses gave Ted a copy of a book about another stroke victim, actress Patricia Neal, that told in detail how she and her husband, Roald Dahl, worked through her illness together. It became a bible for Ted. He stayed with Casey as much as possible during the three months she was confined to the hospital, rushing home in between to help take care of little Kate. One was as helpless as the other.

He had just started shooting *The Womens' Room* and remembers, "I would go during the day to play this s.o.b. insensitive husband and run off at night to be with Casey. It was a crazy time."

Once Casey was back home, she and Ted were surrounded by friends and family, all ready to help.

"My wife is a hell of a lady," Ted says proudly. "She knocks your socks off. Knowing I loved her helped.

I could absolutely see the effect of loving her some days as opposed to coming in other days not loving. I could see the physical result of love, the power of it."

Ted is the first to admit he wasn't perfect during this time. "How can a healthy person really understand what it is like not to be able to move part of your body?"

A person who relied on the support system of the "team," he suddenly found himself taking care of everybody else and nobody taking care of him. "You don't go through that with a halo," he said. "The important thing is you get through it, through to the other side. And as a couple. We'd have these outrageous fights, just trying to clean up all the anger and fears that got suppressed when you were handling the emergency itself. Hers was, 'Where were you?' Mine was, 'You almost died! You said this marriage was forever and ever, you almost died. I don't trust you anymore.' "

The family joke became who would walk first, Kate or Casey. Little Kate won, but two years after the stroke, Casey took her first unassisted steps. Today the only trace of the stroke is a barely perceptible stiffness in her left foot.

It was in Ted's next film, *Body Heat*, that he displayed his distinctive blend of elegance and comedy, playing the horn-rimmed, scene-stealing, dancing district attorney. Aramis cologne for men hired him as the sophisticated spokesman in their upscale commercials, and then Ted got a call from *Cheers* to try out for the lighthearted lady-killer, Sam Malone.

Glen Charles said, "Being sports' fans, we decided our bar owner would be an ex–football player. We actually tested some ex-players, but we finally decided we needed a professional actor for the role. Ted had made an episode of *Taxi* [playing a flamboyant hairdresser] and we saw him in *Body Heat*. He seemed to have just the right blend of humor and character and the right responses for a leading man—except that he was the most unathletic person we tested. So we rebuilt the part to suit him. With his height and build, he could be a baseball player. We concluded that a former relief pitcher would add humor to the show, since some of them tend to be flaky anyway."

Shelley Long remembered, "We tested together for the parts and that was real Tension City. Ted kept saying, 'Oh, gee, I'm not good at improvisation, I'm not good at comedy,' and I said, 'Pshaw, you're a good actor. That's the number-one priority in improvisation.' We did two scenes from the pilot and he was terrific."

Initially, Ted had his doubts about returning to television in a series. The experiences on the soap stages weren't fun, but when he saw the script, he said, "I like the spread between being the reformed alcoholic and being a kind of crazy relief pitcher for the Red Sox. I like being able to play back and forth between those two things—the light and the heavy. You can play the silliness and you've also got somebody who has handled something very heavy in his life, so he's got a lot of empathy for other people and I like bouncing back and forth between that."

The Sam we are most familiar with is the slightly dim womanizer. In the first episode, with very few words, we quickly learned just what kind of man Sam Malone was.

A jilted and stranded Diane Chambers had helped Sam by answering his phone. It's a woman he doesn't want to talk to and he gestures for Diane to take a message. She listens, hangs up, and turns to him.

DIANE: You're a magnificent pagan beast.
SAM: Thanks. What's the message?

The next few years have Diane attempting to raise Sam's consciousness about his constant dalliances with the opposite sex while Sam tries to explain his behavior.

SAM: I haven't had much experience saying "no" to a woman. The closest I've ever come is, "Not now. We're landing."

The writers have given Diane some very "picturesque" descriptions of her version of skirt-chasing Sam Malone.

DIANE: As usual, Mr. Malone has his brains caught in his zipper.

And when Sam tries to say something intelligent, Diane rarely gives him the chance.

SAM: A thought just crossed my mind.
DIANE: A thought can't cross your mind, Sam. The bridge is out.

Not used to rejection, Sam continues to try different approaches, hoping to entice Diane into a quick rendezvous.

SAM: (*to Coach*) I'll be in the back checking the wine.
(*to Diane*) Want to join me? It's empty, and quiet and dimly lit . . .
DIANE: . . . Much like your mind.

"Sometimes I play Sam blatantly dumb," Ted explains, "and I think that's a mistake. Basically, I think he doesn't want to be smart. Especially because who you're gauging him against is Diane, so it's like, no thanks, I'd rather talk straight and communicate than do the verbal trip that she's on. I think Sam's smart enough to keep it an ambiguity whether he's bright or not."

Interestingly enough, for all his supposed mental deficiencies, Sam is one hundred percent businessman when it comes to running the bar. The moments are rare, but if he's dealing with an employee, a friend, or customer who could risk upsetting the delicate balance he's attained in having a popular bar, he doesn't mince words.

In order to heighten the realism of *Cheers*, the producers sent Danson to bartending school so he'd look like he knew what he was doing. "I spent two

Sam calls a meeting in his office. *(Rhea Perlman, Shelley Long, George Wendt, Woody Harrelson, Ted)*

weeks at the American Bartenders School," Ted recalled, "and it was one of the most exciting parts of getting ready for the role. It was nerve-racking to remember the different drinks, the ingredients that go into the drinks, and the garnishes that go on top. To pass the course, you had to do twelve drinks, three at a time, in seven minutes. God knows what they tasted like." Jim Burrows proudly acknowledged that Ted came in second in the class.

During the filming of the first episode, Ted applied all the tricks he'd learned at school, but when he saw the final show, he realized that all his mixing was done behind the counter and none of his deft handiwork could be seen.

For a young man who was once painfully shy around women, Ted Danson is having a ball playing Sam Malone. "I found out that I'd always had a secret hankering, but never the guts, to be him. Playing him gives me the chance to live it out. It's my adolescence. Finally."

31

When asked for his own description of Sam, Ted answered, "He's the American male in flux. I don't think I knew Sam Malone or what he was until about the second year. If I went into a bar and saw Sam, I'm sure I'd strike up a conversation with him. He's willing. I like that he's a jock. I like that he's a womanizer, but also very intelligent. Most of all, I like his willingness to be with people."

After three years of playing genial Sam, Ted went against type to play the father who committed incest in the TV movie *Something About Amelia* and won the Golden Globe award for Best Actor.

During the summer of 1985 he made three movies, back to back: *Little Treasure*, with Margot Kidder; *Just Between Friends*, with Mary Tyler Moore, Christine Lahti, and Sam Waterston; and the Blake Edwards comedy *A Fine Mess*, with Howie Mandell.

Blake Edwards said of Ted, "He reminds me of an early Cary Grant. He has a great comedic facility, along with being a handsome guy. That's hard to find."

Jim Burrows sees Ted "as a character man, not a leading man. That's what he does great. He's a little like Jack Nicholson in that way."

Ted plans to continue working in motion pictures while doing *Cheers* and has recently turned producer, developing the Jonathan Kellerman novel, *When the Bough Breaks*, into a TV movie, in which he also starred.

Wife Casey, an environmental designer, has been working on remodeling their southwestern-style home, and she and Ted have adopted a second daughter, Alexis.

He feels he's grown a lot playing Sam Malone. "I was very sensitive and on the opposite end of macho. Sam gave me a chance to grab my boleros and strut a little."

Sam Malone Fact Sheet

Background: Dropped out of high school in senior year when offered a contract to play Class-A ball

Occupation: Relief-pitcher for the Red Sox, where he first met Ernie Pantusso
Wore uniform #16

Nickname: "Mayday"

Career History: Rookie of the Year
Once struck out Cash, Kaline, and Freehan with a tying run on second
In a doubleheader against the Orioles in 1972, saved both games with seven pitches
Left baseball in 1977 due to heavy drinking
Joined Alcoholics Anonymous in 1979

Family: Brother Derek, hot-shot debonair attorney

Marital status: Divorced, ex-wife named Deborah, no children

Current: Bought Cheers in 1976
Hired Diane Chambers as a waitress in 1982

Health: Hernia operation in 1986

Favorite Color: Blue

Favorite Food: Chinese

Hobbies: Sailing and skiing

Lucky Charm: Bottle cap from last drink he ever had

Shelley Long
as
Diane Chambers

Shelley Long plays the sheltered former teaching assistant, full of book learning but very little knowledge about the real world, who has taken a job as a waitress at Cheers in order to learn more about herself. Coming from the straight world of academia into the melting pot that is Cheers, Diane is both horrified and intrigued by the handsome lady-killer Sam Malone, and not at all certain what to do about it.

When Shelley came in to read for the part of Diane, Glen Charles noticed immediately that "she didn't have to 'reach' as other actresses did. Other actresses would have to assume part of the identity which seemed to come naturally to her. She's very sexy, not in the usual sense of being voluptuous, but there's a certain intelligence, a quality of vulnerability touched with innocence."

"It was funny when I was doing the reading," remembers Shelley, "I could tell from the look on the producer's face that nobody had read the part right. There was one line that was a real toughy. I thought, Boy, I don't know if I can get the laugh on this one. I worked on it for about a week and when I did the audition, the director let out a whoop and yelled, 'Yes.

That's it!' I giggled inside and thought, Yup, I was right. I'm supposed to do this television show."

Shelley Long was born on August 23, 1949, in Fort Wayne, Indiana, to a pair of teachers. Her destiny seemed preplanned, but at age four, Shelley announced that she wanted to be a clown when she grew up.

She enrolled in speech and drama clubs in high school, and in 1967 won the National Forensic League's original oratory championship. "My speech training was fantastic," she recalled. "My speech coach made me aware of where my interests were, what my strengths were, and how to develop them."

To balance things out, Shelley was also a cheerleader. This was "an opportunity to get up and make a fool of myself in front of people."

After two years at Northwestern University, she told her parents that she wanted to pursue a career in show business and dropped out of school. Within a short time, Shelley was co-host, writer, and associate producer of a local Chicago television magazine show on WMAQ, Channel 5, called *Sorting It Out*. She won three local Emmy Awards for her work, and gained national attention when the *Today* program began airing some of her stories.

Shelley missed acting so she signed up for Chicago's famed Second City improvisational workshop. Her talent was noticed quickly and she was asked to audition for the company.

After only six months with Second City, producers Bernie Kukoff and Jeff Harris brought her to Hollywood to do a comedy pilot called *That Thing* on ABC. Shelley's parents were concerned because of all the horror stories they'd heard about L.A., but Shelley had her head on straight and knew this was what she'd always wanted.

The pilot didn't become a series, but Shelley stayed in Hollywood and began working immediately, guesting on such series as *Family*, *M*A*S*H*, *Trapper John, MD*, and *The Love Boat*. She was also featured in made-for-television movies that included *The Cracker Factory*, *A Promise of Love*, and *The Princess and the Cabbie*.

She said of her training with Second City, "When you improvise, you learn a lot about yourself. You observe more. You listen more, but probably first and foremost, you have to know about yourself. You can't help but see what's coming out of your mouth and how you're behaving."

Shelley also attributes that special talent she has for making her characters believable and funny to that training. "Actually all you have to do to be outrageous in almost any setting is to tell the truth. It's so unusual that people are stunned by it."

In 1979 Shelley embarked on a motion picture career and over the next three years would make *A Small Circle of Friends*, *Caveman*, and co-star as Belinda, the reluctant prostitute, in *Night Shift* with Henry Winkler.

After the hectic pace of Chicago, Shelley admits she had trouble adjusting to the slower pace of life in Los Angeles. It meant adopting a whole new life-style, learning to ease up and relax. Oddly, a book on the life of Picasso helped her to get a handle on her own career. She said, "He led a lusty life. He had passions for many things, but it sounds like he had an inner kind of way to a real love, to a total existence. That reassured me. I discovered it's okay to be happy and have a good time with your work."

For a while, Shelley had been feeling confused about her career choices, her strengths as an actress, and the kinds of parts she wanted to play. She clearly had set her sights on a motion picture career when she was sent the script for the pilot episode of *Cheers*. Her immediate reaction was, "I so identified with Diane. I knew who she was and I liked her in spite of her faults. I had to admit I'm supposed to do this. The ideal combination for me is a project like *Cheers* with comedy, drama, real emotions, and real people."

She tested with many different actors, while Ted Danson tested with different actresses. The day Ted and Shelley tested together, something magical happened, and the producers knew they had their Sam and Diane.

Glen Charles has said of Shelley and her character, "Diane has an intelligence which comes through as a certain spunkiness, resilience, and vulnerability. Shelley has all that. Both she and her character share the same zest for life. Both need to feed on people and gain people's approval."

The comparisons of Shelley to Diane are inevitable. Diane, a former teaching assistant, chucked the academic life to become a waitress, and Shelley broke away from a long line of educators to become an actress. Both women are thinkers who can analyze what they're doing and why.

This trait in Diane has more than once left Sam screaming in frustration.

SAM: You always have to think about things. You always have to talk about things. You always have to know what we're doing, why we're doing it and what it means.

In a way, neither Diane nor Shelley has relinquished her past career. Diane is still learning, every day, about herself and the world around her, and Shelley said of her own background, "Once a teacher, always a teacher, and once the daughter of teachers, always the daughter of teachers. That's still there. Teachers share. They get people excited about ideas. Acting is similar in the sense that it's sharing."

Both women have a love of words, but where Shelley will offer a stream-of-consciousness monologue as she thinks her answers out loud, always returning to make her point, Diane tends to ramble and ultimately forget what she was talking about.

DIANE: Carla . . .
CARLA: I know what you're going to say.
DIANE: What?
CARLA: Something irritating and long . . .

Diane knows that her steady stream of talk happens when she's nervous. She compares it to the hiccups, only with her it's uncontrollable chattering.

Shelley admits that Diane has a tendency to take herself a little too seriously, to take life a little too seriously. "She thinks too much, instead of feeling into a situation, instead of using her intuition. I'm learning how to do that better, to get back to a real basic operation, but it's hard."

It seems to be equally hard for Diane, although she does try to join in the free spirit of things at Cheers.

DIANE: Fishing. How lovely. It always reminds me of Tom Sawyer and Huck Finn, innocent boys with fishin' poles. You know, it's truly essential to one's peace of mind now and then to get back in tune with the rhythms of nature, and completely shed the mechanized world.

SAM: (A moment, then) So, Norm, did you remember to bring the TV?

Shelley feels that "Diane grew up with a lot of wealth, and I didn't. That's a big difference. Diane's main focus of her young adulthood, up to the point when she walked into Cheers, had been education and academia—that was not my choice. I do love to think and I love to read. Diane knew nothing about sports, and coming from Indiana, you gotta love basketball in that state or you might as well move. I'm working more actively than I think Diane is to be aware, be aware of myself, be aware of the world.

"Diane is more intellectual than intelligent," Shelley continues. "She's full of inconsistencies. She appears bright and intelligent, but usually she doesn't know what she's talking about."

Diane started as a woman who took herself very seriously, and gradually started to change. She began asking questions about herself and her life.

Between bouts with Sam, Diane had a serious relationship with Dr. Frasier Crane, whom she'd met during a self-imposed confinement in a sanitarium. When Frasier's mother meets her son's lady-love, she feels this analytical barmaid isn't good enough for her "baby." Diane's growth and confidence in herself is evident in a heartfelt speech she gives to Mrs. Crane.

DIANE: I'm sorry if I made a bad first impression on you. I think—no, I know it's a wrong impression. I happen to think I'm one terrific catch. Perhaps I'm a diamond in the rough right now, but I'm a dreamer and I have a little habit of making my dreams come true. For instance, here's a dream I have. When and if I marry Frasier Crane, I will be the kind of wife and person you will be glad to call family. People will get tired of hearing you boast about your daughter-in-law.

Her nemesis, Carla, consistently gets the better of her with her razor-sharp attacks. Diane picks her mo-

41

ments to get back at Carla, as in the case where they are both working together (for a change) to help Sam out of a jam.

CARLA: Hey wait. I just got an idea.
DIANE: You mean you've actually conceived something besides a child?
CARLA: Oooo. A bitter and unprovoked attack. I like it.

But usually, Diane just won't give Sam a break.

DIANE: Just when we were ready to hang a "For Rent" sign on Sam's forehead, a tiny little thought claims squatters' rights.

Even during the time she and Sam were seeing each other regularly, Sam's lack of verbal prowess was a constant source of irritation for Diane, although her attacks were less violent.

DIANE: Oh, my Sammy's putting on his thinking cap. A wee, pointy little thing with ear flaps. (She kisses his forehead) But on you it looks roomy.

Ted Danson has said of working with Shelley, "We're very competitive, or at least I am. It's a double-edged sword, but it's a competitiveness, a toughness that elevates, not denigrates each other's performance. Shelley's definitely a powerful, equal match, and for that, I'm tickled pink." Giving credit where it's due, Danson admits, "When you laugh you're laughing at the writers. They're quick, good . . ." His one request is that they give him ammunition when he's one-on-one with Shelley. "I ask them to make sure my gun's loaded."

In 1981, while testing for the role of Diane Chambers, Shelley Long married stockbroker Bruce Tyson,

whom she'd met on a blind date. Bruce had been playing a charity benefit roulette wheel and won a dinner for four. The couple he invited to join him brought Shelley along. Shelley says she knew he was the right man for her the minute she met him.

And, three years later, during the third season of *Cheers*, Shelley discovered she was pregnant. That same season Rhea Perlman became pregnant with her second daughter, and George Wendt and his wife discovered they, too, were going to become parents. The joke on the *Cheers* set: "Don't drink the water."

When Shelley told the producers, she said, "They were shocked. One came over and gave me a kiss and congratulated me. Another sat there with a grin on his face, and another just sat there stunned."

They ultimately decided to let Rhea's pregnancy show, as it worked for her character, but Shelley's pregnancy would not be visible. Those episodes that heavily featured Shelley were shot out of sequence, early in the season, and those filmed during the later stages had Diane always carrying a full tray in front of her, or standing behind the bar, and after she and Frasier left for Europe, only on the phone, usually bundled in heavy coats and parkas.

By this time in Shelley's career, she had made two additional movies, *Losin' It* with Tom Cruise, and *Irreconcilable Differences* with Ryan O'Neal. Steven Spielberg had cast her to co-star with Tom Hanks in his *The Money Pit*, to begin production in March 1985. When Shelley told him about the baby, he agreed to postpone the schedule for a few more weeks rather than recast.

When asked how Shelley is able to balance the hectic schedule of a weekly television series, movies, husband, and new baby daughter, Julianna, she said, "If there's any one key to that, it's my mental attitude. If you prepare yourself mentally and believe that you can do it—well, I have to admit that I'm sort of dazzled

by all the energy, too. I think more begets more, you know? If you seek to have more and use more, there's more to use. You become tuned in to where you need to be.''

There seems to be more and more of Shelley's philosophy in the character of Diane, too. Glen Charles once said, ''Diane's a victim. Victims are funny because people identify with them. They are real. When she first comes into Cheers, the audience is on her side immediately. They like her. People identify with people who have been buffeted about a bit. At the same time, there's a feeling she can meet all her problems head on. She's going to triumph over all.''

Diane Chambers Fact Sheet

Family: English mother, Helen; army lieutenant father, Spencer; met during the war when Helen was working as a nurse. Family chauffeur is Boggs

Background: Diane was an eight-month premature baby
Parents separated when she was twelve years old
Won merit badges as a Brownie
High school pep squad

Education: Bennington College—studies included pre-law, art, Indian studies, and psychology. Identifies herself as a "Skinnerian Behavioralist"
As of 1985 was working on her masters thesis— she was eligible in thirty-seven different subjects and chose psychology

Pets: Cat—"Elizabeth Barrett Browning" (died 1983)

Early loves: At age nineteen—he went off to boot camp, and when he returned with a crew cut, she never wanted to see him again
Professor Sumner Sloan, under whom she worked as a teaching assistant. They were engaged and on their way to Barbados for the wedding and honeymoon when Sumner left her at Cheers and went back to his ex-wife, Barbara

Current: On/off romance with Sam Malone; Brief affair with Dr. Frasier Crane

Health:	Nervous breakdown; Golden Brook Sanitarium
Hobbies:	Theater and opera
	Stuffed animals, including "Mr. Jammers" (a giraffe), "Freddy Frogbottom" (a frog), and "Mr. Buzzer" (a giant bee)

Love on the Rocks
–with a Twist

The 1980s: An age of confusion about sex roles and stereotypes.

Sam Malone has always found it easy to have any woman he set his sights on, although he made sure these women were interested in the same things he was—sex—and that they were not intellectuals.

Diane Chambers is an intellectual. Upon meeting Sam, her head says, "No, no," while, to her surprise and annoyance, her body is screaming, "Yes! Yes!" and it frightens the hell out of her.

Year One

The first time Sam and Diane met, you knew trouble was brewing. He was intrigued by this brainy, beautiful, and vulnerable lady. She was different from the women he was accustomed to dating, primarily because she didn't seem interested. Diane couldn't help but notice Sam's good looks, self-confidence, and easygoing smile, and refused to acknowledge that she could find herself attracted to such a "cretin."

51

Here were two people, not really meant for each other, but fascinated by each other.

At first Sam attempted coy innuendos, hoping to entice Diane into bed. That failing, he went straight for the kill, bluntly stating his desire to get her in the sack. (Not the way to win a fair maiden's heart, although one imagines that Diane couldn't help but play out the fantasies in the privacy of her room.) Here was a man from the knock-'em-over-the-head-and-drag-'em-to-bed school of romance. His reputation stood on its own. All of the women he'd had and tossed aside were still willing to come back anytime he crooked his little finger. And for that very reason—all attraction aside—Diane became even firmer in her resolve not to be just another entry in his little black book.

Her refusals were amusing to Sam at first, but Diane's constant putdowns made it increasingly more difficult to believe this conquest was really going to be worth the effort. Sam had to endure insults about his IQ, "the intelligence of lint," his choice in women, his clothes, and even his favorite cologne when Diane would introduce him as "Sam, I reek, therefore I am, Malone."

Yet, when either Sam or Diane seemed to be troubled, Diane would initiate a private conversation in Sam's office. She was always a ready and willing friend, and Sam, as much as he appreciated the innocence of her gestures, couldn't resist making a pass or some sexual innuendo, leading Diane to crown him "King of the Single Entendre."

Even though their first year together was filled with barbed banter, a friendship was developing that would be the foundation of their relationship. And, by the end of that year, Diane was willing to make the commitment to a physical relationship with Sam.

Year Two

They've had sex and it was terrific for both of them. If only their personalities didn't get in the way, it would be an ideal love affair.

SAM: What do you think it's like to be attracted to some- one who makes you sick?

It was agony for them, wonderful for us. Sam and Diane were in love, but it wasn't any love they'd read about in books.

SAM: I used to think that the more women I conquered, the more it made me a man. But when I was with all those women I was really just looking for the right one.
NORM: And now you've found Diane.
SAM: Yeah, right. When they made Diane, they broke the mold . . . tried to pretend like it was an accident.

Gradually, their sarcastic barbs were exchanged for lovetalk that bordered on nausea for the Cheers regu- lars. Diane was calling him "Sammykins," and their loveplay moved from the bedroom into the bar. It was not an uncommon sight to see them enter together, laughing and giggling. Diane would draw a water pistol, fire at Sam, and he'd fall down and play dead, saying only a kiss from Diane could revive him. She would gently bend down and kiss her prince back to life.

NORM: I miss the good old days when they threw up at the sight of each other.

With all of their playfulness, there were signs that all was not as perfect as it seemed.

SAM: I thought you weren't going to call me stupid now that we're being intimate.
DIANE: No, I said I wasn't going to call you stupid while we were being intimate.

Hanging around with Diane was making Sam a little smarter. One day in particular, while talking about superstition and Sam's lucky bottle cap . . .

SAM: A lot of good it did me. The only battles I ever won, I won by myself.
DIANE: Sam, that was brilliantly put.
SAM: Yeah, you said that to me a few days ago.
DIANE: I know, but you remembered it and used it in the proper context.

But Diane's praise for Sam could turn cold on a moment's notice, and she'd be back referring to him as a man whose "most valuable life function is supplying carbon dioxide to plants."

SAM: You always think you have to tell poor Sam what to like, what not to like, how to walk and talk, what fork to use for soup and salad. I know, I know, you

54

don't use a fork with soup. It was a mistake. Don't say, "You don't use a fork with soup," please. If you do nothing else for the rest of your life, please don't say, "You don't use a fork with soup."

Sam and Diane know their relationship is over.

There was trouble in paradise, and with Cheers being such a small world, nothing was secret from anyone else. Carla, renowned for cutting to the heart of the matter when referring to Sam and Diane, called them "my favorite couple, Steve and Idi Amin."

By the end of the second year, Diane was on the verge of a nervous breakdown, and Sam was questioning his own sanity at ever having taken up with her.

SAM: I don't know what it is, but it's gotten to where I do stuff I don't even want to do, but just knowing it's going to tick her off, I gotta do it. The angrier I think she's going to be, the more I enjoy it. Is that weird?

And when Diane confided in an artist who was doing her portrait, we realized she had more insight into Sam than she'd let on.

DIANE: Sam happens to have a great deal of intelligence. If you could see behind his coarse facade . . . I admit that Sam and I are different people. Sometimes that's good. Sometimes that's not so good, sometimes it's awful. Sometimes he hurts me and seems to like it, sometimes he makes me feel very lonely. Sometimes he makes me cry, but Sam's very special. He pretends to be dumber than he is. Sometimes as a defense, and sometimes to provoke me.

The painting was a major source of contention between Sam, Diane, and the artist. Diane wanted to believe Sam would like the surrealistic portrait over those of children with big eyes; the artist swore Sam could never appreciate it. Unfortunately, Sam and Diane's last fight of the second season ended with her storming off before he had unwrapped the picture. If she'd only stayed a moment longer. Sam was very impressed with the painting, but no one was there to witness his reaction.

Year Three

It was a rough summer for both Sam and Diane. Sam had returned to drinking, and Diane had herself committed to a sanitarium. While at Golden Brook, she met Dr. Frasier Crane. Here was a man more her equal; an affair ensued. Her self-confidence returned, and comfortable in the knowledge she had a lover to protect her from any stray feelings, she asked Frasier to help Sam with his drinking problem. Frasier knew deep inside that Diane still felt something for Sam, and the only way to deal with it was to push them back together and let it either grow or die forever. He helped Sam and in the process became fond of him, frequently turning to Sam for advice about Diane. Diane wondered why.

Diane and her new love, Dr. Frasier Crane *(Kelsey Grammer)*.

FRASIER: I was hoping for some insight.
DIANE: What insight could you possibly hope to gain from a man whose IQ wouldn't make a respectable earthquake?

Sam assured Frasier there could never be anything between him and Diane again.

SAM: I could get out of prison after twelve years, serve on a ship with an all-male crew for another four and be dropped on a desert island for another three eating nothing but oysters day after day, and if one day Diane came walking out of the surf naked, all I'd want from her is the hockey scores.

You knew these two people wanted to believe what they were saying about each other. There were moments when it looked like the old flame was about to flare, but Diane always managed to put it out when she'd hit Sam with her long speeches—such as after the time she had a disastrous meeting with Frasier's mother:

DIANE: It's not her fault, not having a sense of humor. And if it's not her fault, it's your fault for telling me I didn't have a sense of humor. And if it's not your fault, it's Frasier's fault, for not appreciating my sense of humor. All I know is, it's not my fault. It's all clear to me.
SAM: (As she walks away) A whole year of my life . . .

While Diane continued to see Frasier, Sam went back to dating a different woman every night, and one evening wanted to look his best. He trusted Diane as a friend and asked her advice on what to wear. He probably wouldn't have gotten in trouble if he hadn't gloated so much. Unfortunately, he did, and she got him again.

SAM: Tell me, Diane, when you dream about me, what am I wearing?
DIANE: An ant hill.

Diane refused to allow her feelings for Sam to blossom and pursued her affair with Frasier, only to discover she still called out Sam's name during moments of intimacy. Frasier was her equal intellectually, but he was insecure and a little too pompous. He might have been perfect for Diane prior to her coming to Cheers, but the years she'd spent there broadened her self-awareness and now she found she couldn't quite love Frasier with the same intensity as she had Sam.

She and Sam discussed what went wrong with their relationship, and another side of Sam was revealed.

SAM: I'm sorry, I did the best I could when I was with you. You're right. I have blind spots and I'm not a good boyfriend, but I never tried so hard for any woman. We had a lot of bad times, but the good times with you were some of the best of my life.

Frasier knew it was only a matter of time before he lost Diane to Sam again. In a last attempt to win her affections, Frasier asked her to come to Europe with him for six months while he worked as a visiting scholar. Diane accepted, since Sam gave her no reason to stay. When Frasier proposed, she once again called Sam, hoping for some sign that he still loved her enough to want to stop the wedding. Sam seriously toyed with the idea while Norm summed up their past.

NORM: You and Diane are special people, alone, separate, individually. But together you stink. Your chance of making a go of it together for the long term rivals only that of a spark and a gas pocket. All you two really have going for you is some fantastic sexual chemistry that draws you together and makes your lives miserable. I'm sorry, Sam, but to the casual observer, your running off to Italy would have to seem stupid beyond reason.

But he ran anyway, unbeknownst to Diane. What she never realized was that he was on a plane while she was changing the location of the ceremony.

Year Four

Unable to find Diane in Europe, Sam returned to Cheers never wanting to hear her name mentioned again. Then, the last person he ever expected to see walked in the

A broken man, Frasier resorts to sweeping Sam's floor.

door—Frasier. A broken man, he'd lost his self-respect, confidence, and Diane. She had dumped him at the altar and embarked on a life of decadence throughout Europe.

Frasier told Sam that she was back in the Boston area, doing penance by working in a kitchen for the Sisters of the Divine Severity. For all they'd put each other through, Sam still saw himself as a strong friend of Diane's and couldn't bear to see her throw her life away. He went to the abbey and asked her to return to Cheers.

In the Abbey, Sam tries to stop Diane from screaming.

It was not an easy decision. They gave in to their passion once and drove each other crazy. If Diane agreed to return, they knew they'd be back flirting with each other. They both felt they knew the pitfalls of getting involved, but once again the attraction was very strong. Diane tried to tell Sam what would happen if they renewed their relationship.

DIANE: It would be the Hell where people who misbehave in Hell are sent.

By now, they knew each other so well that they were able to work out their frustrations and offer support by giving the other what he needed. If Sam needed to get angry, Diane would willingly give him cause, calmly sit through his tirade, and then when he was spent, he would thank her. It was her pleasure, and two grown-ups would calmly exit his office.

They finally seemed to be moving toward a healthy relationship in which they could accept each other's weaknesses. Behind the witty repartee there was love and tenderness and understanding.

Sam and Councilwoman Janet Eldridge *(Kate Mulgrew).*

They both began dating others and Diane watched with increasing jealousy as Sam and a beautiful councilwoman began a steady affair. By the end of the fourth season, Sam was so confused he drove both women away. Realizing his mistake, he picked up the phone, dialed a number, and asked the woman who answered if she'd marry him. But the resolution to this cliff-hanger wasn't revealed until the opening show of the next season. Sam had asked Diane to be his wife. For four years Diane had harbored hopes this would happen. Sam planned a romantic evening on the water in a sailboat to ask the question in person. After careful consideration, Diane said, "No."

Also Starring

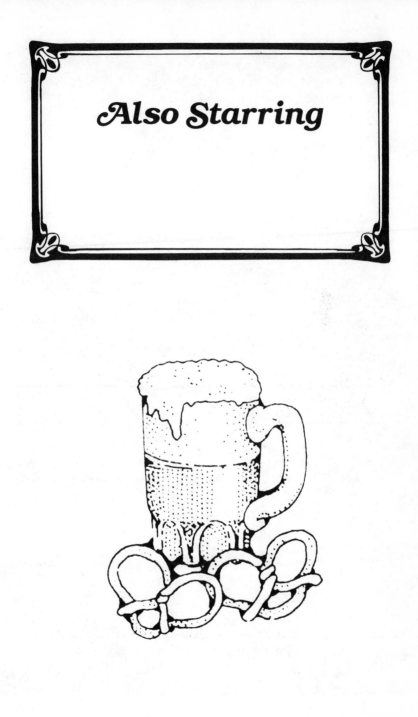

Rhea Perlman
as
Carla Tortelli

One of the joys of watching *Cheers* is waiting for one of Carla Tortelli's razor-sharp barbs.

DIANE: Hi, everybody. Guess why I'm here?
CARLA: Generations of inbreeding?

In real life, actress Rhea Perlman is nothing like her character Carla. She admits, "I never came up with a snappy line in my life." Shelley Long once said, "Rhea is about as far from Carla as she could possibly be. She's quiet, almost shy, and doesn't have any of Carla's angst." Rhea's writer-sister, Heide, agrees, saying, "She has the same earthiness but isn't bitter like Carla."

A sense of humor about the world around her seems to have given Rhea a unique perspective on life. Born on March 31, 1949, in Brooklyn's Coney Island section to a doll-parts manufacturer, her early memories were of her father's warehouse. "You'd go in and see all these little eyes and arms . . ."

Doll-like herself, at a diminutive 5'1" and 100 pounds, Rhea was shy as a child but always thought acting sounded like fun. She enrolled in Hunter College to take drama classes and soon found herself in the mad scramble for odd jobs between auditions for off-Broadway parts.

Nothing ever turned out ordinary for her—even the old standby job of waitress took a left curve when held by Rhea. She had been hired by the posh Rainbow Room high atop Rockefeller Center. She recalled, "It was a very fancy place and they wanted you to be well trained. The kitchen was three flights down from the dining room, and you had to carry this silver tray with all the food on it using only one hand. They had guys posted on the stairs just to make sure you were carrying it that way." After only three days on the job, Rhea's wrist gave way and she managed to dump a trayful of spaghetti on none other than David Rockefeller himself. "They would have thrown me out of the forty-fourth-floor windows if they could have."

If there were awards for the most unusual part-time jobs, Rhea would win hands down. In addition to waitressing, she also worked in a bookstore as an "eraser" —that is, erasing scribbles other people had put into used books so they could be resold, and, for a time, as an allergy tester for an orthomolecular psychiatrist.

Her first acting role was in an experimental play titled *Dracula Sabbat*. She liked to take chances with her acting and one of her most memorable forays into the outer limits was in *Vinyl Visits an FM Station*, a bizarre tale of a Hanoi radio show, which also co-starred her husband-to-be, Danny DeVito.

Rhea first met Danny in 1970 when she went to see a friend in a short-lived off-Broadway play, *The Shrinking Bride*. Danny played a stable boy and captured most of her attention. After the show, she was invited to join the cast for dinner and sat across from Danny. Sparks flew and within two weeks they were living together.

By the mid-seventies, Danny had gotten his break in motion pictures, playing Martini in *One Flew Over the*

Cuckoo's Nest. In 1977 he was invited to direct a movie for the American Film Institute and Rhea came along, offering predictions of gloom and disaster for them in cruel, foreign Hollywood. Her fears were unfounded and she soon was acting in movies and on television. Some of her films include *Mary Jane Harper Cried Last Night, Intimate Strangers, Having Babies II, Drop Out Father,* and *Stalk the Wild Child.*

Danny was working as Louie DiPalma on *Taxi* and Rhea was ready to settle for a life of playing battered women and social workers when she was cast as Zena, Louie's passionate girlfriend for four episodes of *Taxi.*

When it came time to cast the part of Carla on *Cheers,* Glen and Les Charles remembered Rhea as an actress who had always taken her characterization to the fast lane. The character had already been created and they were on the search for an actress who could pull off the hostility and still be likable, and could create the onscreen tension needed between her and Diane Chambers.

When Rhea was called in, she was very nervous. She knew everything depended on this reading. Shelley remembers when she did the scene with her, "I could sense how uptight she was, but we picked up right away on the visual difference between us." Glen Charles said he knew the moment he saw them together that they were right.

When Diane says such lines as, "My dear Carla, perhaps your desperate observations accurately reflect the relationship between men and women in the demimonde which you inhabit, but to those of us who no longer scrape our knuckles on the ground when we walk, your views are incredibly primitive," Carla is perfectly justified in retorting with any one of fifty names she has reserved for Diane. Among them are Pencil Neck, Gozzel Head, Whitey, Bleachbag, Spindle Shanks, Fish Face, Lady Dye-Job, and the Answer Geek. Perhaps not as eloquently stated as Diane's assessment, but equally effective.

Carla has not had an easy life. After attending St. Clete's Academy for Wayward Girls, she married Nick Tortelli. She supported him through television-repair school, and upon graduation, he promptly dumped her, leaving her with the four kids. It's not uncommon for her to arrive at Cheers with an announcement that when she got home the night before she found a grease fire in the kitchen; the kids had started dinner without her.

Despite their marital status, Nick still drops by Cheers to see Carla.

CARLA: What the hell do you want?
NICK: Hey, is that the kind of hello I deserve?
CARLA: No, bend over and I'll give it to you.

Carla has a soft spot for Sam. Although never stated, we get the impression Carla came with the bar. She's seen Sam through his days on the bottle, and off. She respects him as a businessman and an employer, and has hinted more than once that she has a crush on him, although she knows it could ever be reciprocated. Sam genuinely likes her, and only occasionally feels the need to reprimand her for her behavior. A perfect example is the time an obnoxious customer started berating the Red Sox, and Sam in particular, and Carla leaped up, flew across the room, jumped on the man's back, and started slamming his head against the bar. As it was, Sam still defended her.

Carla is appropriately nauseated by Sam's fawning over Diane, and she minces no words when it comes to telling Diane her feelings.

CARLA: I still believe in him. I say he's still got some hair on his butt.

Her sarcasm is usually triggered by the mundane, having learned to take a more realistic look at the world than most. Next to Diane, Cliff, the mailman, is one of her favorite targets.

CLIFF: Clifford Clavin has the soul of a winner.
CARLA: That's pronounced "weiner."

She's especially vicious when it comes to Cliff's pitiful love life.

CLIFF: (To Norm) Hot babe at three o'clock. This may be the next notch on the old Clavin bedpost.
CARLA: The only notches on your bedpost come from banging your head in frustration.

Rhea has said of her character, "I like someone who can say whatever she wants. In real life, I don't always have a shot to get off at somebody I'm pissed at . . . [Carla's] really a good waitress, who's very professional about her job. And she's tough. She doesn't take crap from anyone."

Perlman and DeVito had been living together for eleven years when they decided to make it official. Danny was still working on *Taxi* and they had a lunch-hour wedding. Rhea wore a rented antique lace Victorian gown. "I looked like a wedding cake," she said. Danny rushed home from the set, and to the trilling strains of a recording of Our Gang's Alfalfa singing "I'm in the Mood for Love," Danny and Rhea said their vows in the rain-soaked garden of their home. Rhea said it was the first time her Jewish parents and his Italian parents had ever met. It was over in an hour, and life went on as usual.

Rhea had waited until her midthirties to make the decision to have a family. "When I was younger, there was too much unsettled stuff and financial insecurity in my life. My friends with kids seemed so grounded. I'd retch every time I'd see them with their big bags of diapers."

She wisely hinted to the producers that she could become pregnant during the course of the series. Two weeks after starting work on *Cheers*, Rhea found out she was going to have her first child. When she told Glen and Les Charles, "They weren't shocked at all and we ultimately decided the whole thing was as good for the character as it was for me." Lucy Chet DeVito was born on March 11, 1983.

Carla with ex-husband Nick Tortelli *(Dan Hedaya)*.

For the first couple of episodes of the second season, Rhea wore a pillow to approximate the final stages of Carla's pregnancy, and then, in an episode called "Lil Sister Dontcha," while Carla was in the hospital giving birth to her baby, Rhea had the treat of playing Annette, Carla's "good" sister. The fifties-style hairdo and sweet naiveté were such a contrast, it took many viewers a little time before they realized Rhea was playing the part.

Two years later, Rhea became pregnant with her second child, Grace, born in 1985, and once again, it fit in perfectly with the character of Carla.

Most of us remember Carla's preoccupation with talking about the hassles and horrors of raising kids, but one of these speeches stands out for its pathos. The following occurs in an episode where ex-husband Nick has taken their oldest son to live with him and his new wife.

CARLA: I may not be the best mother in the world. A lot of times I think those kids are gonna drive me nuts. But when [Nick] came and told me he wanted one, something happened inside of me. I realized those kids are just about all I have and as much as I hate to admit it in public, I like them. I didn't think losing one would hurt so much, but it does.

Rhea once confided, "I'd been listening to Carla talk for so long, I wasn't sure how I'd react as a mother. I was afraid I wouldn't be a good one or I wouldn't enjoy spending so much time with an infant. Now, I want to have nineteen children! That's not true, but I really am kid crazy."

Carla Tortelli Fact Sheet

Background: Carla Lozupone attended St. Clete's Academy for Wayward Girls

She and Nick Tortelli used to dance on *The Boston Boppers,* a local TV show similar to *American Bandstand*

Marital Status: Divorced from Nick Tortelli; wedding reception was held in a bowling alley

Carla worked as a waitress to put Nick through television-repair school. As soon as he graduated, he dumped her

Family: Six children: Anthony, Gino, Lucinda, Seraphina (while married to Nick); Ann Marie (fathered by Nick in a moment of weakness after divorce); Ludlow (fathered by Dr. Bennett, Frasier Crane's mentor)

Hobbies: Sports fan of any Boston team

Favorite Hobby: Blacking out teeth on *Vogue* covers

Special Skills: Ability to repair anything from televisions to toilets

Nickname: "Muffin"

Favorite Food: Chicken McNuggets

Favorite Movie: *Lady and the Tramp* (in particular the spaghetti-eating scene)

Religion: Catholic; goes to Mass every Sunday

Nicholas Colasanto

as

"Coach" Ernie Pantusso

The lovable bartender always a beat or two behind the rest of the world was played to perfection by the late Nicholas Colasanto.

According to the *Cheers* producers, the inspiration for Coach was "a little Yogi Berra, Sparky Anderson, and Casey Stengel." Glen Charles elaborated, "These were certainly not dumb men; they just had a different perspective on things. We tried to make Coach not so much stupid as indecisive and pursuing his own line of reasoning. Behind the seeming stupidity was a sweetness and innocence and a striving to make sense out of life.

The producers had auditioned between fifty and seventy-five actors, including Sid Caesar, looking for that special quality that would make "Coach" come alive. Glen Charles said, "Nick was our first choice from the very first time we saw him."

Nicholas Colasanto had not started out to become an actor. Born in 1923, Nick was one of seven children in a family of Italian immigrants living in Providence, Rhode Island. After a five-year hitch in the navy during World War II, he returned to school and got his accounting degree from Bryant College in Rhode Island.

77

He spent the next three years as a bookkeeper, and in 1951 was ready to accept an offer with an oil company, in Saudi Arabia when something happened that changed his life forever.

He saw two Broadway shows and was bitten by the acting bug. Nick said, "It was like catching a virus. I saw Charles Boyer in *The Red Gloves* and Henry Fonda in *Mister Roberts*. I discovered that it was what I wanted to do for the rest of my life." He went home and discussed it with his mother, who gave him her blessing, saying, "Well, go be an actor. Do you want to spend your life adding up all those boring numbers?" Nick continued, "I chucked everything at twenty-eight and enrolled in the American Academy of Dramatic Arts."

He later admitted it wasn't a very rational act. He had already used his G.I. Bill for college and now found himself having to work at a succession of odd jobs to support himself. Ironically, in addition to being a waiter, dishwasher, and short-order cook, he also spent time working as a bartender.

To his dismay, he was not invited to complete the two-year program at the Academy. "I was called into the office and told that I had some sort of rough-edged talent for acting, but that they thought there was no room for me in any theater. Maybe they were right, but it made me angry and goaded me on. It made me more determined to become an actor."

His professional acting career began in Phoenix, Arizona, earning $25 a week plus room and board as an apprentice at the Sombrero Playhouse. From there he went on to regional theater and summer stock, which eventually brought him full circle—back to New York.

In 1956, Colasanto was cast in the co-starring role opposite Ben Gazzara in Broadway's *A Hatful of Rain*. Even though he received rave reviews, other parts were hard to come by, and for the next eight and a half years he eked out a living as a director and acting coach at New York's prestigious Actor's Studio.

His performance in *Across the Board on Tomorrow Morning* won him an Obie nomination in 1962, but Colasanto was becoming disillusioned with Broadway. "Things got very lean in New York. Tennessee Williams' and Arthur Miller's careers had begun to wane," Colasanto explained. "What was left were the British imports and wonderful brassy girly musicals—and I'm not brassy or beautiful. In fact, there is no theater in New York anymore. There's a very prosperous thing called Broadway."

Three years later, his longtime friend, Ben Gazzara, who was then starring in the very successful TV series *Run for Your Life*, sent Nick a cashier's check for $1,000. There was a note attached saying, "Get on a plane to L.A., and have a drink on me." Nick packed his bags and headed for California.

By this time, Nick had decided that he was better suited to work behind the cameras, and set out to learn the tricks of the trade from TV directors such as Mark Rydell and Leo Penn. When Nick felt he was ready, Gazzara insisted that he be given a directorial assignment on *Run for Your Life*.

His career soared and he collected over 100 credits directing for series such as *Bonanza*, *The Streets of San Francisco*, *Columbo*, *Hawaii Five-O*, and *The Name of the Game*. He occasionally appeared in front of the cameras in guest spots and was featured in the 1980 film *Raging Bull* as the Mafia chief. But it was in the role of Coach on *Cheers* that Nicholas Colasanto became a star.

Nick had almost given up acting entirely when his agent suggested he read for the part of Ernie Pantusso. Nick said at the time, "It was a long stretch from [the Chief] to the Coach, but I read for them and connected."

Nick once described Coach as "terribly naive and not particularly well educated. He had many happy years in the baseball dugout. Ernie is a composite of a

lot of easygoing, wonderful guys in my old New York neighborhood who worked with their hands and backs."

COACH: I think of smart things and by the time I say them, they come out stupid.
CARLA: That doesn't make any sense.
COACH: Well, you should have heard it before I said it.

There was a childlike innocence to Coach, a literalness combined with a willingness to believe in what he saw. This was aptly demonstrated when he was shown a business card from "Professor Tony—I can teach a dog to sing."

COACH: It's true, everybody. There's a picture of a dog with notes coming out of his mouth. This guy must be good.

"We have absolutely lucked out with all of our cast," reflected producer Glen Charles. "Each one has taken his character further than we thought he could go. That was certainly the case with Nick. Among other things, he was a great listener—Nick as an actor and in the role. The character was somebody all the other characters could explain things to, and we could always cut to Nick for a silent reaction. When another character did a joke and we needed something to break up the laughter, we'd cut to Nick because as Coach he was always trying to make sense of what was going on."

Nick once said about Coach, "He's innocent and sweet, but not dumb. He may be intelligent, but he's not worldly-wise. He's so positive. That's what makes him funny."

His confusion about banks, for example, isn't that different from ours.

COACH: Like, why do they call them tellers? They never tell you anything. They just ask questions. And why do they call it interest? It's boring. And another thing, how come the Trust Department has all their pens chained to the table?

One of his most memorable characteristics was the way he would draw a blank about some fact while listening to a conversation. For several minutes he would knit his brows, knowing the answer was somewhere in his memory. When he finally recalled it, he would invariably blurt it out in answer to a totally inappropriate question.

His memory lapses were attributed to his having been hit once too often on the head by a baseball. In an early episode, he explained to Diane that this was an art form.

COACH: I perfected it when I was with the St. Louis Browns organization. I could get hit by the pitch and take my base anytime I wanted. I tried to edge my body in front of it. Sometimes I took it right in the old melon. I was a master of it. (He hands Diane a ball) Here. Try to miss me.

After much prodding, Diane finally does throw the ball "far and wide." The audience hears a "thunk" and all the customers applaud. Norm tells Diane she got him "right in the old honeydew. He had to dive for it, but he still got it." Sam confirmed this, saying, "He's the best."

Coach is polite to a fault, even to the point of answering rhetorical questions.

DIANE: Coach, you know the way Sam always complains that I'm not spontaneous?

COACH: I think so. He goes (à la Sam; gesturing with his hands) "Diane, why can't you be more spontaneous?"

Or . . .

DIANE: When Sam comes back, will you tell him something?
COACH: Sure will. Goodnight, honey.
DIANE: Wait. I didn't tell you what to tell him.
COACH: Oh, I'll think of something.

Coach was, without question, the father figure of the group, whether it was keeping Sam on the wagon, helping Diane through a nervous breakdown, or sympathizing with Carla over her family. He was the perfect sounding board for everyone's problems and they could count on him not giving away secrets—since he tended to either mix up or forget almost immediately what he'd just been told. His innocence and desire to understand made it impossible for him to be judgmental. And just when you thought he'd never say anything that made sense, exactly the right words would pop out of his mouth to set everyone back on the right track.

For example, when a woman he had fallen in love with suddenly came into a lot of money and dumped him, he responded with a wisdom that surprised everyone.

COACH: I know this isn't you talking. It's the money. This is just something you have to get out of your system. Just remember the look in these eyes, because you'll be seeing dollar signs in everyone else's.

One episode revealed a darker side of Coach. He had accepted an offer to manage a Little League team and, before our eyes, the playful, easygoing Coach turned into a tyrant, with his entire team threatening mutiny. Ultimately, we learned that his striving for team perfection was simply Coach doing what he thought was right. Sam gently reminded him of a teacher Coach once had who had bullied and embarrassed him in front of the whole school. Coach still hated that man, and when he finally made the connection between that and how these young boys were going to feel about him, he did an immediate about-face. The Coach we all knew and loved was back, and the boys were about to be treated to a very special human being.

Nicholas Colasanto was a small, unassuming man. The praise the producers had for Nick was barely outmatched by his love of the *Cheers* family. He has said, "I'm an extremely happy man who loves to go to work every day on *Cheers*. We've got great writers, producers, and a group of actors who care, with Ted Danson setting a relaxed pace and atmosphere. There is none of that 'star business' here, which I've seen on about seventy-five percent of the sets I worked on as a director."

At an NBC press party given on the *Cheers* set at the end of the first season, everyone wanted to sit on Norm's bar stool and interview Ted and Shelley. No one seemed to be paying much attention to Nick, who stood at the bar sipping a club soda, and he didn't seem to care. One reporter asked him if he was upset by the lack of attention. His response: "Are you kidding? This is fun. I'm having a great time. What can I tell you about Ted and Shelley? They're really wonderful people, you know."

Toward the end of the third season, Nick was absent from five filmings. He had had a history of heart trouble, had spent two weeks in the hospital, and was currently home recovering. The scripts explained Coach's absence as a vacation; in one episode, Sam tells Diane, "He's getting his driver's license renewed. That means he's probably lost, driving somewhere in Maine." Nick stopped by the studio on Friday, February 8, saying he was feeling much better and should be back at work to film the season's final episode in March. The following Tuesday, February 12, 1985—filming day for *Cheers*—the terrible news was delivered. Nicholas Colasanto had passed away at home that morning.

A stunned cast and crew closed the set, canceling that evening's show.

For three years in a row, Nicholas Colasanto was nominated for an Emmy as Best Supporting Actor in a

Comedy Series, and the press reacted as strongly to the death of Coach as they did to the death of Nick. It was a beautiful tribute to an actor that he had made Ernie Pantusso so real that the world mourned his passing.

Tom Shales, TV Critic for the *Washington Post*, summed it up in his column: "Television can foster the most intimate kind of friendships and we'll remember Coach as the actor played him: someone who wished none of his fellow beings any harm. There are such people on the planet. You're lucky to meet them on the street or on a TV screen, either one."

The Thursday night following Nick's death, NBC ran a special episode of *Cheers*. It opened with a photograph of Nick with Ted Danson's voice announcing: "This encore presentation of *Cheers* is dedicated with love and appreciation to the memory of Nick Colasanto."

The episode chosen was "Coach's Daughter," in which Coach has to face the painful truth that his daughter is marrying an obnoxious lout because she doesn't feel she's beautiful enough to warrant any better. He's at a loss as to what to do until Sam reminds him of an old baseball story in which the key booster phrase was "Go get 'em." Fortified, Coach has a long talk with his daughter, convincing her she is the most beautiful girl in the world and doesn't have to settle for less in a man. Triumphant, he turns to Sam, "Hey, Sam, I got 'em!" Sam smiles and agrees, "You got 'em, Coach." Indeed he did.

The last episode ("Rescue Me") starring Nicholas Colasanto aired on May 9, 1985. The season cliff-hanger was filmed out of sequence because of Shelley Long's pregnancy, and for the audience, it was a loving reminder of Nick and "Coach."

"Coach" Ernie Pantusso Fact Sheet

Family: Ernie Pantusso's parents had been drinking Chianti the night he was conceived

One brother, three sisters, and a dog named Smiley

Background: In high school, he was chairman of the prom committee, although he himself never graduated

He joined the navy at Pensacola and spent six months in the brig after getting in a fight on shore leave

Occupation: Catcher for the St. Louis Browns (later the Milwaukee Brewers)

Coached Double A in Pawtucket

Pitching and third-base coach for the Boston Red Sox, where he met Sam Malone

Marital Status: Widower; his old navy pal, Walter Deitweiler, introduced him to Angela, who became his wife

He was married thirty years before Angela passed away

Children: One daughter, Lisa, who lives in Pennsylvania and works as district manager of a men's suit company

Politics: Democrat—and he drives an American car

Nickname: "Red"—not for red hair, but because he once read a book

John Ratzenberger
as
Clifford C. Clavin, Jr.

Next to Ted Danson and Shelley Long, John Ratzenberger, who portrays the trivia-spouting mailman, probably receives the most fan mail of any actor on *Cheers*.

"There are Cliffs everywhere. I don't know how many postal workers have told me they have one in their local branch," John said.

Originally hired for just seven episodes, John wound up working in twenty-one of the first twenty-two shows and has been in every episode since. He said, "It took me about a year to relax and accept the fact that I was wanted. I kept thinking somebody would tell me to stop hanging around, and every once in a while I thought about sneaking off the set so nobody would have to be embarrassed when I was canned."

When John was called to audition, it was just to play "one of the guys at the bar." He was handed three pages of script, and gave a perfectly good reading for a character named Norm. He could see the producers weren't bowled over by his performance enough to pick him from the dozens of actors reading for the same part. On his way out, he had one of those sudden flashes of insight that he's learned to trust over the years. "I hit them with the notion that every bar has a sort of wise guy who thinks he's got the answers to everything. Without waiting for a response, I immediately went into a little improvisation about the kind of guy who loves uniforms and useless information. Well, they loved it and they laughed just enough to give me the job. The best bunch of writers in the business took over and," John said, "Cliff was born."

John Ratzenberger was born on April 6, 1947, in Bridgeport, Connecticut. His Hungarian father provided John with a slightly skewed view of the world. John remembers him as a man "who used to interrupt dinner, sailing through the kitchen doing a Jack E. Leonard impression, twirling his hat as he went out the door. Sometimes he even came back. At six o'clock on Sunday mornings, he'd put a Louis Prima–Keely Smith album on the hi-fi, more than loud enough to roust all of us out of bed. Well, how could you have a real dour outlook when you're surrounded by characters, including your own father, from day one?"

He gives credit to Sister Regina at his Catholic grammar school for his impeccable comedy timing. "[She was] a hawkeye. When I was able to make my friends break up without getting caught by Sister Regina, I knew I had a future in show business."

He attended Sacred Heart University, majored in English, studied karate, became an archery instructor, and, in his spare time, joined the drama club. At Sacred Heart he made his stage debut in Tennessee Williams' *Summer and Smoke.* Cast as an understudy, he was asked to take over the starring role twenty-four hours before the play's first performance. Additional roles in *West Side Story* and *Waiting for Godot* sufficiently whetted his appetite for the stage.

After graduation, with no other work in sight, John

had decided to take a job on an oyster boat off New Haven when several of his old college chums came down to the dock. John was wanted to replace the lead actor in a production of the comedy *Luv* at the Stowe (Vermont) Playhouse. John not only did the play, but stayed on as artistic director for the season. For the next two years, John remained in Vermont working as a blacksmith and carpenter. He decided to take a three-week vacation to England, liked it, and stayed for ten years.

An old college pal, Ray Hassett, showed up one day, and he and John decided to resurrect some of the old acts they had done together at Sacred Heart. They figured what worked for college kids might work for the Britishers. They formed "Sal's Meat Market" and began doing their act in pubs around London. The Arts Council of Great Britain bestowed on them the first grant to an American act to tour Europe. John not only performed, but also co-wrote and directed their sketches.

"It was character comedy," explained John. "I never pretended to be a leading-man type. We'd do stuff like having the setting as a shipping dock of an atomic plant where my partner was addressing a group of workers and I played 'the group,' a one-man crowd moving around the stage, using different mannerisms and voices."

They built quite a large following over the next five years, until Ray had to return to the States. John stayed on in England and started acting in films. "Whenever they needed somebody to play an American soldier, they called me." John Schlesinger first used him in *Yanks*. As with any starting actor, film roles were few and far between. John was forced to take any job he could to keep body and soul together, and there were times that a ketchup sandwich constituted the main meal of his day.

Upon returning to the United States, he got his Screen Actors Guild card when cast as a member of a sick rock band in the film *Motel Hell*. To date, John's films include *A Bridge Too Far, The Ritz, Superman, Superman II, Ragtime, The Empire Strikes Back, Outland,* and *The Falcon and the Snowman*.

It was upon returning from England where he played Candice Bergen's jeep-driver in *Gandhi* that he was called in to read for *Cheers*.

It was at that audition that John recalled a character he used to do back in London with Sal's Meat Market: "He was based on a cop I know in my hometown. He was a nice guy but a know-it-all. It was never important to him whether his answer was correct; the only thing that counted was giving a fast answer with a lot of confidence behind it."

Originally, Cliff was going to be a security guard, but two days before filming the first episode, the producers decided to change him to a mailman. It was felt that a mail carrier would have access to all sorts of magazines and periodicals and that's where he'd picked up all his trivia.

Glen Charles says of John, "He's an improviser. In terms of Cliff spewing trivia, we typically supply just the start of it in the script, then John takes it off into orbit."

John's years of touring Europe with an improvisational group, plus a number of arcane scientific journals that he subscribes to, give him ample ammunition for creating the very believable Cliff, obsessed with useless information.

CLIFF: Due to the shape of the North American elk's esophagus, even if it could speak, it could not pronounce the word "lasagna."

Since Boston is Cliff's beat, it is only natural that he would know all about his city.

CLIFF: Boston is the hub of the greater Boston Area, which numbers some two and three-quarter million people spread out in eighty-three cities and towns. It covers 497 square miles and it weighs approximately two and a half million tons.

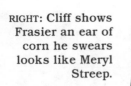

RIGHT: Cliff shows
Frasier an ear of
corn he swears
looks like Meryl
Streep.

Norm Peterson is Cliff's best and probably only friend. Norm accepts most of Cliff's trivia spouting as gospel, but will look at him in horror when Cliff brings in vegetables that Cliff thinks resemble Meryl Streep and Richard Nixon. Cliff, in other words, is Norm's safety net.

NORM: Cliffy, you're kind of a handy guy to have around. Just when I think I've gone off the deep end, I look over and there you are . . . diving off the cliffs of Acapulco.

Yet Norm always defends Cliff.

NORM: I know you all think he's a weird guy, but in his defense, he'll probably never reproduce.

There is a depth to Norm's friendship with Cliff that only rarely surfaces, such as the time Norm had to tell him that the woman Cliff had chosen to love was a tramp—a valuable lesson in friendship, honesty, and trust.

And once, when Cliff was too sick to finish his postal rounds, Norm offered to substitute for him and was arrested for mail theft. Cliff was torn between explaining to his superiors what had happened so Norm could be released from jail, or keeping quiet so as to not lose his job. He openly admitted that being a mailman was his whole identity; but when it came down to losing that or his best friend, he risked his career to save Norm.

John has based his characterization of Cliff on the typical guy in uniform—a man who, as soon as he puts on the uniform, takes on heroic qualities. "Cliff is the kind of guy who wishes he'd been a combat marine, but maybe he was nearsighted or had flat feet so became a mailman. He loves the respect he gets." Cliff believes he's the postal-service equivalent of a Green Beret.

But, for all his macho swaggering, Cliff is a complete washout when it comes to women. Sam Malone is his idol, and more than once, Cliff has been allowed to gingerly touch Sam's little black book. For Cliff, these moments are a near-religious experience.

John feels that "Cliff is like the construction workers who whistle at women but turn to a quivering mass when they're face-to-face with a woman. The greatest fear of these men is that they won't live up to their expectations."

CLIFF: The roots of physical aggression found in the male species are in the DNA molecule itself. In fact, the very letters DNA are an acronym for Dames are Not Aggressors.

But something happens when he is confronted by a pretty woman.

CLIFF: Pleased to do you . . . I mean, how do I meet you . . . I mean . . .
NORM: Smooth, Cliff.
CLIFF: I hate her.

Carla is relentless in her pursuit of rapping Cliff, especially when it comes to his incompetence around women.

CLIFF: You ever heard of the lone wolf, Carla? The lone wolf, c'est moi. A man by himself, needing no one. I touch no one, no one touches me. I am a rock. I am an island.

CARLA: You am a boob.

Norm feels for his friend whenever Cliff says something stupid. It probably wouldn't bother him if no one else heard, but someone usually does, and that someone usually is Carla and she always has something to say about it. Norm will turn to Cliff and in all sincerity ask, "Why do you say things like that?" Cliff will answer, apologetically, "I didn't know she was there."

"The most challenging thing I have to do with Cliff is to show him intimidated by women," says John. "I grew up with two sisters—one older, one younger—and I've always been comfortable around women. In fact, one of the reasons I stayed in England ten years is that I was a bachelor then and there's no Puritan ethic there— remember, the Puritans left to come here."

Like Cliff, John Ratzenberger is himself a man with considerable awareness (mostly firsthand knowledge) on everything from deep-sea fishing to making wrought-iron grillwork. "John loves to go exploring," explained Glen Charles. "He's curious about all kinds of things. More than anybody I know, he'll go into a new town and just snoop and sniff his way around."

John and his wife Georgia relish trips to places like Sioux City, Iowa, where last summer they discovered stores full of Heartland Americana. John says he "likes real wood. Something you can carve your initials in." He loves driving across the country, looking for home and farm sales. "Somebody else buys things at the sale thinking it's junk, but a lot of it is real collector's items."

John's scavenger tendencies led George Wendt to observe, "His car had all these dents from strapping things like old dresser drawers to the roof."

John feels all these things may be gone in another twenty years. "The regional differences in this country are going—the accents, the customs, the way people live are all becoming so similar. I think it's an absolute shame."

These days it's getting harder and harder for John to quietly cover the country. He's recognized everywhere he goes, and finds himself inundated with requests to speak at gatherings of actual postal personnel. In 1985 he did a commercial for the U.S. Postal Service.

When asked how he feels about his sudden notoriety, John replies, "All the *Superman* movies and other things I did were to pay the rent. This is it. This is what I ate ketchup sandwiches for all those years."

Clifford C. Clavin, Jr.
Fact Sheet

Background: Father abandoned him at the age of nine, and to this day, Cliff still lives with his mother

Marital Status: Single

Occupation: Postal carrier; assigned to the South Central Branch, Back Bay Station Voted Postman of the Year—one of 267 winners in the greater Boston area

Car: Studebaker

George Wendt
as
Norm Peterson

The beer-chugging accountant with the dead-pan delivery who observes life from a bar stool is played by George Wendt.

"When George first read for a part in *Cheers*, the character was named George," recalled Les Charles. "He was supposed to come in, have a beer, and stay all night."

George still remembers that first cast reading with director James Burrows: "It was at that session that the characters of Norm and Cliff were really set. It had already been decided that Cliff would be in uniform. We thought a blue collar barfly would be too much of a chiché, so we made Norm white collar, but not too distinguished. He became an out-of-work accountant, which is a pretty neat trick to pull off."

When asked why he thinks the producers chose him for the role, George will proudly point to his ample stomach and say, "This."

But there was much more to it than that. Les Charles said of George's droll readings, "Some guys throw away lines; he throws away his whole performance."

It took George Wendt a lot longer than most young men to discover what he wanted to do with his life, and unlike many of us, he was lucky enough to get the chance to do it.

Born on October 17, 1948, to a Chicago investment broker and realtor, George was second in a brood of seven brothers and sisters.

"It was a little frustrating," he said, "because my two brothers didn't come along until I was almost out of the house, so I wound up turning my sisters into halfbacks and quarterbacks while running plays through the house."

At age thirteen, George was sent to an exclusive Jesuit prep school in Prairie du Chien, Wisconsin, "to be groomed for success. I didn't particularly want to go, but our neighbors all sent their kids there and they went on to become doctors."

He was accepted at Notre Dame, but after the strict prep school, he commented that Notre Dame was "like Sodom and Gomorrah to me." It was "party time," and the week of his finals, when a friend called and invited George to go visit a friend at another college, he didn't hesitate to say yes. "I was due to take my finals the next day, but I thought, what the heck, so I went along, figuring to spend a few hours with the guys."

It turned out the other college was in Denver, a thousand miles from Notre Dame, and George ended up staying for two weeks, missed all his final exams, and received a 0.0 grade-point average for the semester. "I wasn't very focused at the time," he understated.

In 1971, George did finally receive a B.A. in economics from Rockhurst College in Kansas City, Missouri. Its admissions director was from his old prep school and George confided, "I'm sure he broke every rule in the book to get me in."

With no career goals in mind, George decided to "drop back fifteen yards and punt." That translated to traveling throughout Europe and Africa on five dollars a day. "The three big occupations were doing your laundry, brushing your teeth, and writing postcards."

Periodically, when he'd run out of money, George would return home to Chicago to work in his father's real estate office. "I wasn't setting the business world on fire, although after a year or so, I was okay with the Xerox machine and getting coffee for the secretaries."

George's father was supportive throughout these indecisive years. George recalled, "I was into the hippie thing and had hair down to my butt. I think it dawned on him then that I wasn't going to take over the family business. But since I've chosen a career, he has always been in my corner."

After about two years, George had had enough. "I used the process of elimination: I went down as many occupations as I could think of—teacher, doctor, accountant—trying to figure out 'What don't I hate?' I'd gone to see Second City in Chicago a lot during my college days, and I thought, Boy, that looks like I wouldn't hate it. And I'm pretty sure they get paid. It was the first time I had any inkling of being determined to do anything in my life."

George enrolled in a Second City workshop and one year later, in 1974, was hired by the company as a "professional satirist." George said of those times, "It was what I liked to do, not what I figured I could do best." George stayed with Second City for six years, time enough to be fired, rehired, booed off the stage, and meet Bernadette Birkett, a fellow comic, whom he married in 1979.

It was while he was with Second City that George learned the art of dead-pan delivery. Everyone there had to memorize the famous Elaine May edict: "Never let them catch you trying to be funny."

NBC did a pilot featuring Second City players called *Nothing but Comedy*. It never sold, but it brought George

Wendt to the attention of NBC executives. With their encouragement, he and Bernadette moved to Hollywood.

The first six months in Los Angeles were deadly for them both. George was quickly cast in guest roles on various shows including *Alice, Soap, Hart to Hart,* and *M*A*S*H,* but he recalled, "I was so wired after the high pressure, gung-ho atmosphere of Second City, that doing two days on a sitcom and that's it for six months was traumatic. I went kind of crazy; I holed up in the house for months like a hermit, sitting around in my gym shorts watching TV." Bernadette finally snapped him out of it. "I was turning into just a lump," he said.

Film offers began to come in and George's motion picture credits began to mount. He appeared in *My Bodyguard, Jekyll and Hyde—Together Again, Airplane II,* and *Somewhere in Time.*

Eventually, George was cast in the part of the coach in a new Gary (*Family Ties*) Goldberg series, *Making the Grade.* At the same time, Glen and Les Charles were casting *Cheers* and remembered George's work from a bit part he did on *Taxi* as an exterminator. They called him in, and even though he was already involved in another series and might not be available for the full season, they figured they could work around his schedule. As it turned out, *Making the Grade* was not picked up, and Norm became a full-time regular on *Cheers.*

One of the moments *Cheers* fans wait for is Norm's entrance into the bar. Each week he has something to say that lets us know exactly how he's feeling.

COACH: What's going down, Norm?
NORM: *Das Boot.* Let's drink to those poor devils.

Or . . .

COACH: What's shakin', Norm?
NORM: All four cheeks and a couple of chins . . .

Or . . .

COACH: How's life, Norm?
NORM: Ask somebody who's got one.

Or . . .

SAM: What's up, Norm?
NORM: My nipples. It's freezing.

Over the years, we've learned a little about Norm. He was a virgin when he married his high-school sweetheart, and to avoid being called a "wuss" by his pals

105

has made a habit of self-deprecating humor and knocking Vera every chance he gets.

For example, when Cliff asks if Norm has ever thought about dying in the act of love, Norm replies, "She claims I do." There is a reason why he and Vera have no children.

NORM: I can't.
COACH: Aw, that's too bad.
NORM: I look at Vera and I just can't.

What we learn by the end of the first season is that Norm is deeply in love with his wife and that she obviously understands his need for a place like Cheers.

Norm's wife Vera always knows where she can find him.

It is clear that Vera already has a child in Norman. When he and Cliff get together, their humor is usually that of seven-year-olds, exemplified by an episode in which Diane is telling Sam of a telephone prank she and her girlfriend used to do in the fourth grade. It involved calling up a stranger, saying they were with a radio station, and "for a trip to Hawaii, name three cars that start with P." The obvious answers are Pontiac, Plymouth, and Porsche. They laugh and say, "No, they start with gas!" And hang up. Shaking their heads with disgust at the moronic story, Cliff and Norm watch Diane and her friend.

But that's not the end of it. Later, in the same episode, the camera cuts to the pay phone in the hall. There are Cliff and Norm, each taking turns making the practical-joke call.

Diane has difficulty concealing her annoyance with Norm and Cliff's often childish behavior, and when she accuses them of making contests out of meaningless issues, Cliff is the first to defend their actions.

CLIFF: On the contrary, Diane. We also address ourselves to some of the most vital and meaningful issues of our time. For instance, if Southeast Asia were to be destroyed by nuclear weapons tomorrow, Norm here would have to push a peanut up Boyleston Street with his nose.

NORM: Only to the corner. Come on, peace.

When Vera throws Norm out of the house, he bunks down at Cheers.

George Wendt has a few things in common with his character: he likes beer and sports, but George doesn't hang out in bars. And he has a terrific home life. He has a suburban soul, and when it comes to living in trendy Los Angeles, George admits, "I sort of feel out of it in terms of haircuts and clothes. I like a little bit of Peoria." John Ratzenberger says George is a "legendary barbecue chef."

George's household consists of Bernadette and her two sons, plus a new baby daughter. He feels all his years of partying in school are getting paid back in full. His evenings are now spent helping the boys with their homework.

In addition, no one could have predicted George's thirst for knowledge based on his school years. George Wendt reads a minimum of four newspapers daily, plus magazines like *Sporting News* and the *New Yorker*.

George said, "Newspapers are in my blood. My grandfather was a superstar of yellow journalism. The equipment he used to take the famous hidden-camera photograph of the [1929] execution of Ruth Snyder is in the Smithsonian."

Ratzenberger says all of this reading has turned George into "Paul Bunyan with the soul of Bertrand Russell, a very easygoing guy with a finely honed intelligence, which I didn't realize until he whipped my kiester in Trivial Pursuit."

Because both John and George came from a heavy improvisational background, no one knows what to expect when these two get together. The NBC network uses them frequently for promotional happenings. George explains, "Ratzenberger and I have complete trust in each other. We get away with murder at these events. We're just like the Katzenjammer Kids."

Some of the bits they improvise during rehearsals end up in the shows. One such case had Cliff and Norm, sensing a confrontation at the other end of the bar, look at each other, shout, "Dive! Dive!" "Aaooogah! Aaooogah!" and then, in sync, they slowly sank out of sight.

For a man who does enjoy a beer in the evening, George says consuming all those glasses on *Cheers* is really a chore. "You see, it isn't beer. It's Near-Beer, which to the best of my knowledge, has no alcohol. It doesn't come in kegs, so the crew pours cases of the stuff into a rigged soda dispenser on the set.

109

"This is done early in the day and the stuff is warm and flat by the time shooting begins. When they first filled the glasses, the cameraman yelled that he couldn't see any foam. Then they started putting a half teaspoon of salt into the empty glasses to create a head. It tastes disgusting. That's how I make my money. That's acting."

During *Cheers* hiatus time, George continues to make movies, and has had major roles in *Fletch* as the unsavory hamburger-stand proprietor "Fat Sam"; in *Gung Ho* as the assembly-line worker who has a hard time adjusting to the Japanese way of doing things; and in *House* as the neighbor of a Stephen King–type novelist whose stories come to life.

Even with all these credits, George is still hailed as "Norm!" wherever he goes. "I get a lot of free beer. The waiter usually arrives with one and says it's from the table over there. Then I look over and all these people are raising their glasses. It's nice."

George acknowledges that *Cheers* fans are a strange breed. "You get these people that you'd swear would not be fans, guys who look like brain surgeons, midforties with salt-and-pepper beards and horn-rimmed glasses. It's curious. They'll come up to you and tell you how much they love the show. That surprises me because they're not the typical persons that would clamor over a TV actor."

George Wendt has created a character in *Cheers* who strikes a familiar chord in millions of viewers who have a favorite home away from home. Now when people ask George, a man who once didn't want to work for a living, what line of work he's in, he replies, "I tell them I sit at the end of a bar, drink beer, crack jokes, and talk about sports. They say, 'The man's a genius.' "

Norman Peterson Fact Sheet

Background: Dean Acheson High
Wrestling team
Graduated 30th in his class
On Audio-Visual Squad (setting up
the movie projectors in class)

Marital Status: Married; Vera, no children
Vera was high-school sweetheart
Norm was a virgin when he married

Occupation: Accountant
In 1960s he sent a dollar to a church
advertising in *Rolling Stone*, and now
he's a licensed minister in the Church
of the Living Desert

Car: Honda Civic

Hobbies: Beer and sports

Nickname: "Moonglow" (earned when a wrestling opponent pulled down Norm's
trunks during a match in high school)

Woody Harrelson
as
Woody Boyd

The young bartender from Indiana who dropped by Cheers to meet his pen pal, Coach, and was hired by Sam, is played with innocence and honesty by actor Woody Harrelson.

Named after his Uncle Woodrow, a Texas rancher, Harrelson's is a true Hollywood overnight success story. His co-starring role on *Cheers* is only the third professional part—first ever on television—that he's played.

Born on July 23, 1961, in Midland, Texas, Woody Harrelson was the second of three brothers. His family moved several times, finally settling in Lebanon, Ohio, when he was twelve. He once described himself as "hyper and a little weird, starting out in kindergarten in Houston, where I kept getting thrown out for fighting. By the time we moved to Ohio, I was looking for a fresh start. Well, the first thing I did in school there was befriend an ostracized girl named Charlotte, who had leukemia. I was the only one who'd sit with her at lunch, so I immediately got ostracized, too. So much for the fresh start."

Woody first discovered the thrill of audience approval when he did his imitation of Elvis Presley on a tabletop in the school library. His classmates cheered and even the dour librarian admitted he was good. Woody said, "That's when it dawned on me that performing might be fun, and I started studying acting."

Very close to his mother (she and his father were divorced), Woody always followed her lead. It was at her suggestion he attended Hanover College in southern Indiana, where he majored in English and Theater Arts, performing in school presentations of *Bus Stop*, *Love's Labors Lost*, *Inherit the Wind*, *Cat on a Hot Tin Roof*, and *The Madwoman of Chaillot*.

After graduating in 1983, Woody and his best friend, Clint Allen, moved to New York with the same high hopes all young actors have. Woody had bought a sky-blue polyester suit that he said "people still rib me about." Clint had been accepted at Juilliard, and on their first night in New York, they were "initiated" by having their car towed away. Woody said, "It kind of went downhill from there as my money disappeared in a hurry. I wound up living in a tiny three-room Hell's Kitchen apartment with five other guys for ten months while looking for an agent."

He found part-time work, but recalled, "The biggest struggle the first year was just holding *any* job. I kept getting fired." After fourteen months of living in New York without getting work as an actor, Woody had just about given up.

"I had borrowed from everybody I could borrow from. There was no more borrowing. I was so frustrated and so upset. I remember thinking there was no way I could live. I had done auditions, good auditions. I had been close on several things, but I couldn't afford to live in New York anymore. I decided I was going to leave in a week to go back to Ohio."

It was then that Woody received a call to be an understudy in Broadway's *Biloxi Blues*. Woody said, "It

116

changed my life. Lots of people don't like to be under-studies, but me, I was ecstatic. I was hanging out with a great group of guys, the guys in the cast. I was making this money that to me was just huge. I sent money to my mom and paid all my debts."

After only six months with *Biloxi Blues*, Woody was cast in a feature role in the Goldie Hawn film *Wildcats*. He learned a lot from Goldie about dealing with star-dom and fame during the five weeks they spent filming in Chicago. He remembered, "People would mob her. It was like they couldn't believe she was Goldie Hawn. You couldn't keep the people away. I asked her how she handled it. She gave me her undivided attention. She said, 'I usually don't. I usually stay home and cook for the kids.' She was just like an ordinary woman with a job."

He had barely finished his work on *Wildcats* when the casting director of *Cheers* spoke with Woody's agent about a new character they were adding to the cast. Woody was brought in to audition for a character named, of all things, Woody.

117

Because he had worked nights in the theater, Woody had never even seen *Cheers* when he went in to meet the producers. He recalled, "I guess if I had watched *Cheers* for years, I probably would have been terrified. But those people were so welcoming. I never felt like an outsider. They said they wanted a farm boy for whom things went right over his head. I said, 'Well, hey, no-o-o-o problem.' "

Woody was called back three times before the producers made their final decision, and Woody Harrelson was cast in the prime, but awkward position of replacing Coach. The first thing Woody did was call his mom and tell her she could stop working, then they both started crying.

Woody's unfamiliarity with *Cheers* probably spared him the realization of just how difficult it would be to replace an actor as well loved as Nicholas Colasanto. "It took me a long time to really realize Nick had been there for three years and the effect that might have on the others." It became clear one night when Woody met a friend of Nick's and she told him she had been unable to watch the show because it was so hard to see Woody in Coach's place. It upset him, but also gave Woody an

even deeper appreciation of the cast and production staff and the warm welcome they had given him.

The producers had stated emphatically that the role of Coach would not be recast with another actor. They knew anyone would suffer by comparison, and went for a totally different look. They did decide to retain the childlike honesty that was a Coach trademark.

Woody Boyd takes everything at face value. Nothing absurd seems to surprise him. He accepts everything. It would never occur to him that somebody might be lying or even telling a small fib. For example, when Cliff gets caught laughing at a man's drink order, he quickly covers saying he was just remembering that morning's comics in the paper. He bluffs his way out of a fight, and a few minutes later, a laughing Woody comes over to him. He wants to know what happened with the rest of the comic strip.

Woody says of his character, "I see Woody Boyd as a naive and innocent type of person who hasn't been tainted by the world yet. Most kids are overwhelmed by sexuality. I think that's something that hasn't reached him yet." As far as comparisons to himself and his character, Woody replied, "I'd say any character has some piece of you in it. I don't consider myself similar to Woody. But there is a part of me in Woody. He's wide-eyed and has a fresh outlook. I have a pretty fresh outlook, but not *that* fresh. Not after living in New York for a year."

Woody Harrelson admits he's never known an adult like Woody Boyd, but he's a character he finds easy to play by merely remembering the innocence of his own childhood. "I just play youth and enthusiasm and a lot of naiveté."

However modest Woody Harrelson is about his talent, the special ingredient he brings to Woody Boyd is clearly visible when you see the simplicity of the words

119

on the script page and remember the genuineness in Woody's delivery.

SAM: Would you mind going down to the wine cellar and getting some wine?
WOODY: Heck no, going down there reminds me of home.
SAM: Your folks have a storm cellar?
WOODY: No, stairs.

Or, as in this example, when Diane was letting Sam know her life was full without him.

DIANE: As a matter of fact, I have a wonderful evening planned. My date, Gregory, and I are going to the theatre, and then to a late night supper and dancing.

WOODY: Boy, does that bring back memories.

DIANE: Oh? Are you recalling a similar evening, Woody?

WOODY: No, I just remembered your date called and cancelled.

This innocence inevitably leads to comparisons to the character of Coach. "It's uncanny sometimes," said John Ratzenberger. "The character, Woody, has turned out to be so much like a younger version of Coach. During a rehearsal or a taping, the attention will shift to Woody and he'll be out there somewhere in the ozone, in a world of his own, just like Nick used to be. And everyone gets hysterical with laughter. But then you also think, Whew, that was so much like Coach, man, it's like Twilight Zone time."

Ted Danson has felt the same thing. "I think it comes with the territory somehow. When I met Woody the person, he wasn't like that. But then one day it dawned on me that it was like having Coach's son on the set. Woody just kind of fell into it."

Woody insists he's not trying to copy anybody. "I'm certainly not trying to do Nicholas Colasanto's character. I know that a lot of lines written for me are Coach lines, but I don't know how Coach would have done them."

John Ratzenberger feels certain Coach would have approved of Woody. He said, "Woody, the actor, plays the fool on the show, but he's certainly no one's fool. Backstage he fits right in. He can be downright silly, but as I say, it's not because he's anyone's fool."

During the course of the fourth season of *Cheers*, Woody's character grew at alarming rates. We were

introduced to a naive farm boy who didn't seem to have any life experience. Several episodes focused heavily on Woody's character. One revealed he had a girlfriend back home, and to avoid talking about the obvious sexual feelings they had for each other, they ate continuously. Since Woody had been in Boston, both he and Beth had lost a lot of weight—until the guys at Cheers popped for a ticket for Beth to come and visit. Suddenly they both began eating again, while Diane, Sam, Cliff, and Norm tried to help Woody face his feelings about Beth. Woody was on his way to becoming a man.

Another episode had Woody gambling. Sam was not about to let Woody throw away his life savings on a long shot, and did not place the bet Woody entrusted to him. The long shot came in, and Sam had to tell Woody the bet wasn't placed. Instead of being angry, Woody was moved to tears. Sam's caring about him was the nicest thing anyone had ever done for him. To appease his own guilt, Sam forced Woody to get angry. It was here we saw that Woody's no dummy. If Sam wanted him to feel he was owed something, fine, he'd take Sam's prized Corvette.

This wasn't the only time Woody surprised Sam. Once, after hiring a second bartender, Sam realized he was going to have to let one of them go. Woody was the obvious choice. Woody didn't make it easy on Sam, but agreed to leave. Sam felt terrible, and as Woody walked out the door, the other bartender told Sam he had been offered a better job. Sam never anticipated Woody would be so tough to woo back. Woody knew he had Sam over a barrel.

SAM: Gee, Woody, is there anything I can do, anything I can offer you?
WOODY: A fifty-dollar-a-week raise.
SAM: Fifty dollars!
WOODY: Fine.

123

Yet, to Woody, Sam is his best friend, father, confessor, and adviser all rolled into one. He would never intentionally say or do anything to hurt him.

Woody Harrelson's celebrity has just begun to be a reality for him. Early in 1986, Woody went to a rehearsal of *All Is Forgiven* to watch his old friend Carol Kane. Sitting in the bleachers he realized, "I was part of a huge network production myself. It occurred to me that this is a *big deal*. On *Cheers* I've been on the set with people I'm comfortable with, people who've become friends, and I've been so caught up in the work that it didn't quite dawn on me what it all really means."

For the "hyper and a little weird" kid from Midland, Woody has found his niche. Recently a girl came up to him and said, "I dearly loved Coach. I never thought he could be replaced in any way, and I was ready to resent anybody who tried. But *you*, you're just strange enough to bring it off."

Woody Boyd Fact Sheet

Background: Grew up on a farm in Hanover, Indiana Always wanted to be a bartender in a big city, and wrote to everyone, asking for advice. Coach is the only one who answered him and they became pen pals

Love Life: Girlfriend back home is Beth Curtis

Best Friends: Used to be the Twilley Brothers until they made a pass at Beth. Now it's the gang at Cheers

Family: Mother still in Indiana; Woody sends tape-recorded messages home; she writes him letters from his dog

Pets: His dog, Truman

Current: Woody came to Boston to meet Coach, and Sam hired him to work at Cheers Polite to a fault, he calls everyone Mr. or Miss

Sports: Very athletic, enjoys racquetball and basketball; won trophys for bowling, but after an accident where he maimed a man with his ball, will never pick up a bowling ball again

Kelsey Grammer
as
Dr. Frasier Crane

The pompous, insecure psychiatrist is deftly portrayed by Kelsey Grammer.

CANDI: You have a cute forehead. Didn't anyone ever tell you that?

FRASIER: No, usually it's I have acute anxiety.

By the third season, the producers of *Cheers* decided it was time to bring a new man into Diane's life—someone who seemed more her equal socially and intellectually. They created Dr. Frasier Crane, a psychiatrist Diane would meet during her self-imposed stay at the Golden Brook Sanitarium.

In contrast to most of the cast's heavy comedy background, Kelsey had a more formal theatrical background. "Casting directors seem to picture me in three-piece suits," he admits, although his work on *Cheers* has shown him to be a superb comic actor, holding his own with the best of them.

The son of professional musicians, Kelsey was born on February 21, 1955, in St. Thomas, U.S. Virgin Islands. Raised in New Jersey and later in Ft. Lauderdale, he attended Pinecrest Preparatory High School.

127

It was in junior high that Kelsey had his first exposure to theater. He was feeling the loss of his grandfather, who had helped raise him, and was given an assignment to read *Julius Caesar*. The teacher presented Brutus as a stoic, defining his philosophy as, "Don't let events step on your spirit." It struck a chord with young Kelsey. "It shaped my personality," he says. "I was a bit of a loner, an outsider. I was invisible."

He joined the drama club and discovered that once he began appearing in school plays, other kids in school noticed him. "People said hello in the halls. I became everybody's best friend."

In contrast to the button-down image of Frasier, Kelsey's first love is surfing. When it came time to make a career choice, he knew he couldn't surf forever, and since acting was his second love, he enrolled at Juilliard in New York City to study theater arts.

After two years at Juilliard, he moved to California, where he could indulge in both of his passions, surfing by day and performing in classical plays at San Diego's Globe Theatre by night.

At his agent's suggestion, three years later he returned to New York where he acted in off-Broadway productions of *A Month in the Country*, *Macbeth*, *Plenty*, and the Obie Award–winning *Quartermaine's Terms* before moving up to a co-starring role on Broadway in *Othello* with James Earl Jones and Christopher Plummer.

Producers in Hollywood were aware of his work and calls started coming in for him to return to the West Coast to work in television. He appeared in two miniseries, *Kennedy* and *Washington*. In addition he also starred as Dr. Canard in the daytime drama *Another World*.

From this auspicious background, Kelsey Grammer was cast as the new love interest on *Cheers*. Even Kelsey admits, "Frasier is such a boob. I look at the shows, and I can't believe it."

Frasier's first encounter with Diane involved breaking up a croquet match between her and a little old lady. Diane was just about to bean the woman with her mallet when Frasier stopped by. Diane evasively summed up the incident saying, "He stopped to correct a flaw in my swing."

Frasier fell helplessly in love with Diane, but knew that deep in her heart she would always be in love with Sam. He tried everything he could to win her over, and had Diane never met someone like Sam Malone, he would seem the ideal man for her. But Frasier paled next to Sam, as much as Diane wished he didn't.

Frasier's deepest insecurities relate to acceptance by other people. He's never been one of a group. As a child, Frasier admits he was always "odd man out."

They'd pick a girl to be on the team before they'd pick him. He was such a wimp, the other boys used to take off his pants and throw them under a passing train.

As an adult, things haven't changed much for him. He wants desperately to be "one of the guys." When Sam Malone invited him on a fishing trip, Frasier was ecstatic. We watched with a little sadness as all the regulars sent Frasier off on a "snipe hunt," then left him alone in the woods while they returned to Cheers. Diane was aghast that they could do this to him. When Frasier finally showed up, he was exhilarated. He felt bad because he hadn't found a snipe yet, but he was going to go back out and not return until he'd bagged one. Diane begged Sam to tell him the truth—that there was no such thing as a snipe—but Frasier looked so happy, Sam couldn't. He and the other guys agreed to go back with Frasier and help. Just when Diane (and we, watching) was ready to write Frasier off, he surprised us. He wasn't as dumb as we'd thought. It hadn't taken long for him to realize what they'd all done to him. Getting them to go back in the woods was his way of getting even. While they remained beating the bushes for a snipe, Frasier planned to sneak back and fix Diane breakfast.

Frasier knew it was only a matter of time before he lost Diane, and at the end of the third season he invited her to come to Europe with him. Because Sam gave Diane no reason to stay, she accepted, and shortly thereafter, Frasier proposed marriage. To his delight, Diane accepted.

At the end of the summer, we learned that Diane had dumped Frasier at the altar. The ultimate rejection had occurred in his life. He lost not only his love, but his professional status and his money. With no place else to turn, Frasier showed up at Cheers. Here, at least, was someone with whom he could commiserate—Sam. An interesting situation developed: two men who had shared the same woman, and that same woman still very close by. Frasier was still hopelessly in love with Diane.

FRASIER: I'll forget about her when the moon turns to ashes and the birds sing nevermore.

And Sam, just because he was Sam, knew he could have her anytime he wanted her. Diane was in the middle, still very attracted to Sam and liking Frasier only as a friend, which served to drive Frasier deeper and deeper into his depression.

Kelsey admits that someone like Frasier Crane is completely foreign to him. "I've always been the inappropriate man in real life. I'm a rake, a vagabond." Kelsey also considers it ironic that he plays the conformist, while Ted Danson, playing the rogue Sam Malone, is so rooted in his personal life.

Kelsey seems to have found a home at *Cheers*. He says of the rest of the cast, "They couldn't be nicer. A bunch of normals. The kind of guys you could sit around a construction site with."

Kelsey currently lives near the Pacific Ocean with his young daughter, Spencer, and sums up his career in surfing metaphors. "You don't conquer a wave—you ride it and sometimes there's a wonderful outcome. The day is right; everything is in tune; you are at your best. The return is extraordinary."

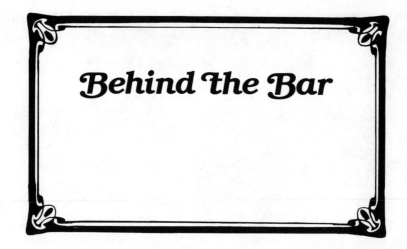

Behind the Bar

Glen Charles, Jim Burrows and Les Charles.

It is Thursday night and we've settled into our favorite chair to watch a little television. At 9:00 P.M. the familiar opening words to the *Cheers* main theme song is heard and we smile, anticipating the half hour to come.

Actually, after adding up the time for opening credits, commercials, and closing credits, we see only about twenty-four minutes of original material. Twenty-four minutes of dialogue that has been honed to perfection by the writer/producers; nuances that the actors have discovered during hours of rehearsal; and split-second editing and sound mixing that, when done properly, should not even be noticed by the viewing audience. All too soon—much too soon—we are watching the end credits roll. The show is over, and it will be another seven days before we are treated to that special feeling *Cheers* brings into our homes.

While we wait a week, over two hundred people work ten to fourteen hours a day putting together that next episode. It takes five working days to rehearse and film a half-hour comedy show. Some productions start their work week on Monday, filming on Friday. Others, like *Cheers*, film Tuesday nights, the new week beginning Wednesday morning.

WEDNESDAY: Ted, Shelley, Rhea, John, George, Woody, and Kelsey arrive at stage #25 a little before 11:00 A.M. There is hardly any discussion about the previous night's filming. That was yesterday—today begins an entirely new episode. Up one flight of stairs, in a large conference room next to the control booth, they help themselves to hot coffee, tea, soft drinks, or juice as the producers and writing staff assemble, arms laden with copies of the new script. Guest actors for this week's show are introduced. Sometimes they're old friends and there are welcoming handshakes and backslapping, but only for a moment. There will be plenty of time to catch up and visit after the ritual reading.

Guest Tip O'Neill hoists a brew with Norm.

The cast sits at one end of the long table, the producers, director, and writers at the other, as the scripts are passed around. All during the previous week's rehearsals, this new script has been written, rewritten, and polished, ready for this read-through with the actors. There will be no ad-libbing or clowning around since this will be the first time that the staff has heard the script read aloud, and they have to know if it works. There is a moment of preparation, then director Jim Burrows reads the opening stage direction. The script supervisor, Gabrielle James, begins clocking as the actors read their lines. Inevitably, there will be spontaneous laughter as the new dialogue is heard for the first time, and Gabrielle will carefully note the elapsed seconds. Within half an hour the entire script is finished. The writers now know what is going to work and what isn't, if it's too long and needs to be cut, or if the entire teleplay has to be scrapped and rewritten from page one. Fortunately for everyone, there have only been a couple of shows that had to be completely rewritten in the five years *Cheers* has been on the air.

Cheers co-creator and director Jim Burrows.

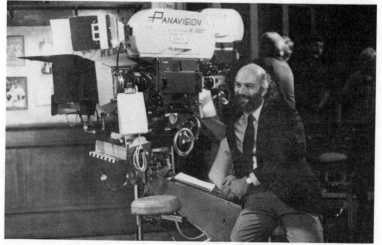

The cast is given a two-hour lunch break while the staff heads across the narrow studio street to the *Cheers* office to begin the grueling task of rewriting.

The office buildings on the Paramount lot are the original two-story bungalows built in the early 1930s. Entering Building D is like stepping back in time. A front stoop with shrubbery planted on either side leads up to a narrow vestibule, off of which is a long hallway with doors on both sides. Framed color photographs from *Cheers* episodes decorate the walls. A narrow staircase opens on another hallway, more photographs, and a large sign that reads CHEERS—IN THE BACKROOM. Small nameplates hang over each door identifying the occupants within. Old fashioned hand-crank windows open either to Gower Street or, across the hall, a view of stage #25. Window air-conditioning units balance precariously to ward off the intense California summer heat, and tucked in the closets are individual electric heaters to be brought out when the cold winter months arrive.

The staff makes its way to writer/producers Peter Casey and David Lee's office, since it's the only one large enough to hold everyone. Gathered are: Peter and David; Glen and Les Charles; director Jim Burrows; David Angell; executive story consultants Cheri Eichen, Bill Steinkellner, and Janet Leahy; story editor Phoef Sutton and staff writer Jeff Abugov; production executive Richard Villarino; and the writers' secretaries and assistants.

Each writer will review any notes he made during that morning's reading. Jim Burrows will add his suggestions, and at the end of two hours, he can go back across to the stage to begin rehearsing those scenes that worked and the writers can begin to rewrite those which didn't.

If all goes according to plan, the actors will have the revised blue-colored pages before they go home that

138

evening. On those occasions when there is extensive rewriting, the actors are sent home early and the writing staff may work to as late as two o'clock in the morning to have new scripts ready for the cast the following day. The times this happens are especially tough on the actors and director as they literally lose one precious day of rehearsal and have to start the read-through process all over again on Thursday.

THURSDAY: Rehearsals begin by 10:00 A.M., with the cast grouped to read through Wednesday's revisions. Then Jim Burrows begins the task of getting the show "on its feet"—that is, deciding who is standing where and what they should be doing. At this point, the actors may have suggestions about their individual characters. Because of the heavy improvisational background of so many of the cast, they are given freedom to try something that occurred to them during the reading and to explore the inner feelings behind the clever dialogue. *Cheers* is a team effort. The ultimate goal is to do the best show possible, and egos are put aside as Burrows accepts or rejects these ideas.

Back in the offices, the writers work feverishly to get the following week's script ready, while on stage #25 the actors begin the tedious task of memorizing dialogue that may or may not stay in the show. Because not all of the cast is in each scene, they have all devised ways of keeping busy during the long spells they are not needed on the set. Richard Villarino believes that the cast has gone through about a dozen different board games from chess and checkers, to Scrabble and Trivial Pursuit, to help keep the energy high during these long rehearsal sessions.

Shelley Long, who is in practically every scene, will find time to slip into her dressing room to meditate or play with her young daughter. George Wendt, his oxford shirt hanging loosely over his jeans, is the show's practical joker, and a warning to newcomers is "Don't let George near any water balloons." John Ratzenberger, when not building miniature golf courses out of waste cans and other props lying around the stage, can usually be found talking about his two favorite subjects: Americana and sailing. An incurable night owl, Kelsey Grammer will disappear either to catnap or indulge himself playing classical music on a piano the producers put in his dressing room. Woody Harrelson, *Cheers'* new "heartthrob," can usually be found reading or shooting baskets with Ted and George on a small court near the stage, and Rhea Perlman will spend as much time as possible with her two daughters, Lucy and Gracie. Because of the "baby-boom" at the studio—not just among the casts of *Cheers* and the other Paramount series, but among their staffs and crews as well— Paramount has installed an experimental day-care center, allowing working mothers and babies to be near each other.

Ted Danson is the "anchor" on the *Cheers* set. If tempers become short when a scene isn't working or the tension needs to be broken, Ted is the man who usually puts everything in perspective again. His easygoing manner and dedication to his work establish a mood that everyone can easily adapt to. It's tempting to goof off when you've had to sit for an hour waiting for your turn "at the bar," but instead of director Jim Burrows, it's usually Ted's voice that calls out, "Okay, everybody, back to work."

That's not to say that Ted doesn't get into his share of mischief. Very competitive, Woody was made to order for equally competitive Ted, and water pistols became the order of the day. Within a very short time George and John joined in, upgrading their "weapons" to Uzi machine water-guns. They've been known to carry their water fights into the studio commissary, dousing more than one innocent bystander. When Jim Burrows took away their toys, they immediately discovered that sticking a hose into a bag full of water gave them great firepower and distance, too. When that was taken away, they could always resort to the seltzer bottles that decorate the bar. Burrows eventually had to give up and reconcile himself to working with a sopping wet cast.

Around five o'clock the production staff will once again assemble on the stage, this time in director's chairs pulled up facing the bar, to watch a complete runthrough of the show. Now the actors are all business as the script supervisor times the action. The ultimate hope is to have a tight twenty-four minutes, but at this stage, they are usually running six to ten minutes over, sometimes more.

Nick, John, Rhea and George try out new dialogue.

One of the joys of working on a show like *Cheers* is the laughter. It's common to hear the writers laughing out loud as words they've been slaving over come to life

141

in the hands of the incredibly talented actors that make up the *Cheers* cast. But not all of the lines will work and, not for the last time, the writers will retreat to their offices to work on those bits and pieces that still aren't to their satisfaction, often staying until the wee hours of the morning until they feel it's right.

FRIDAY: This is the last day Jim Burrows will have to work with the cast on their performance. Similar to Thursday, Friday is a day of rehearsals and memorizing the new dialogue the writers worked on the night before. Each new revision is printed on a different-colored paper to help keep track of the most recent changes. Depending on how many different changes the script has gone through, copies may begin to look like a pastel rainbow. Friday mornings the actors are handed a brand-new pale yellow script, incorporating all the recent changes.

Postproduction on a *Cheers* episode involves not just the editing, but the sound mixing as well. Often during the live filming there can be a noise, either a cough from the audience, a camera wheel squeak or, a dropped prop backstage that will cover a line or word of dialogue. Sometimes, happily, it is even the laughter and applause. Unhappily, these lines get buried on the sound track and need to be rerecorded.

Tim Berry, *Cheers* postproduction supervisor, has to work around the rehearsal schedule to try and snatch the actors away long enough to have them redo a line that will later be edited into the final show. The ADR (Additional Dialogue Recording) stage is like a small theater, but with only a podium and microphone for one actor instead of rows of seats. Tim will have script pages with the dialogue that needs to be redone marked for each actor, and a black and white print of the episode marked where each line is needed. The actor will watch the screen in front of him and try to lip-sync his voice with the action. Through a pair of headphones he can hear the way the line was originally read, and then he must try and duplicate the energy, tone, and volume. Once Tim has these lines on tape, they are taken back to the editors, who work them into the sound track of the show. Listening to the final edited version, it is almost impossible to tell when the *Cheers* actors have had to rerecord any dialogue.

Ted and Rhea at work.

By Friday evening, the script is pretty much the way it will be shot on Tuesday. The actors know they will still get changes, but hopefully only a line or two and not an entirely new scene.

The *Cheers* cast and staff get weekends off, and the actors, when not busy with personal appearances or other publicity-related activities, usually spend them as any of us do—with family and friends.

Members of the cast and crew often get together in their spare time, and a weekend can find John Ratzenberger, for example, when he's not out sailing, helping Kelsey move into a new home. This particular weekend John had offered the use of his van, and he and Richard Villarino helped load all of Kelsey's furniture and boxes, then drove off toward the Marina with Kelsey following on his motorcycle. As John and Richard turned onto the San Diego Freeway, they saw Kelsey pass the off-ramp as he continued on the Ventura Freeway, now heading in the wrong direction. Their last sight of him was the top of his helmet as he sped by on the overpass above them. "Kelsey rides a motorcycle like a bat out of hell," Richard said, grinning. "He must have gone two miles out of his way, turned around, got back on the freeway, and still caught up with us in less than seven minutes."

One season, *Cheers* put together a softball team consisting of some of the crew and Woody, John Ratzenberger, and Kelsey. They were quickly challenged by the *Entertainment Tonight* team. *Cheers* was just out for fun, but *ET* was out for blood. *Cheers* lost but challenged *ET* to another game and won. When word got out that the *Cheers* team had beaten *ET*, other show teams from all over Hollywood began calling to challenge *Cheers*. The team eventually broke up, but not before proving themselves apt sportsmen.

MONDAY: Mondays are reserved for "camera blocking." By now the cast have their movements down pat, and the four cameras are brought onto the stage. In order to get a selection of camera angles to be used later in editing but not subject the audience to watching the same scenes done over and over with one camera filming from different positions, a multiple camera technique is used (the same one pioneered by *I Love Lucy* in

1951). Jim Burrows' job at this point is to decide where each camera needs to be during each scene to capture the full set and the close-ups of the different actors involved. The cast will walk through a scene for John Finger, the Director of Photography, then the stand-ins will take over the tedious chore of literally standing in each actor's place while the lights are set and an assistant director marks the floor with tape. Jim and John decide which camera will be picking up which angle as an assistant cameraman puts a corresponding piece of tape on the floor for the camera operator. During one scene, the cameras may change positions many times to cover all the action that takes place. The final result is a carefully choreographed "ballet" as the cameras silently roll from mark to mark.

TUESDAY: The day starts out as any other, with the cast arriving around noon to complete any blocking not finished the day before. If any last-minute changes were made to the script, these pages are also rehearsed and blocked. A final rehearsal in which the show is done straight through happens around four o'clock and still the cast is receiving small changes in the dialogue. By six o'clock everyone is starting to gear up for the long night ahead. There is no time for a leisurely dinner break. A production assistant is sent out to pick up takeout dinners for the cast. This will be a *working* meal. New lines still need to be memorized, and each member begins to go into that special place actors go prior to giving a live performance. Some may "run lines" with each other; others will go off alone to prepare.

Outside Paramount Studios, an excited audience is lining up on Gower Street. These are people who came by early that morning to pick up tickets for the show. *Cheers* does not hand out advance seating—it's first come, first serve. The ticket window opens at 10:00 A.M. Tues-

145

day morning, and often by eleven, the 239 available seats for that night are gone.

Inside, on stage #25, at 6:45, the cast, having finished dinner, starts going into the makeup room. It is here that director Jim Burrows has one last reading, only this time there is no writing staff present. It's just the director and his actors. They go through the entire show verbally, while makeup people, hairdressers, and costumers make final adjustments to their handiwork.

Seven-fifteen and the audience is now seated. Among them, but never introduced, are usually Ted's wife, Casey; Shelley's husband, Bruce; Georgia Ratzenberger; Les Charles' wife, Zora; and Linda Burrows. Mary Ann Charles, Glen's wife, and Danny DeVito with his two babies prefer to sit up in the booth, behind the audience.

There are no curtains covering the set, and the audience can observe the entire *Cheers* bar with Sam's office off to the side. A small band plays in a corner of the bar, welcoming them into the now-familiar pub. J. J. Wall, the "warm-up" man, is entertaining the audience by telling stories, answering questions, and, in general, loosening everyone up for the evening to come.

At seven-thirty the actors line up backstage, ready to begin the show. The band plays a little introduction music, and J.J. introduces the cast of *Cheers* to eager applause.

Ted Danson is aware of the special magic that he and Shelley create on camera. "We come from totally different acting backgrounds, but something happens on Tuesday night when we do the show for a live audience. It's difficult to describe, but there's flirting, one-upsmanship, healthy competition, and mutual trust. We absolutely relax and have a good time."

The next three hours seem to fly by. J.J. keeps the audience entertained between costume and set changes. Most audiences would be fidgeting after three hours of sitting, but when asked if they would stay for a few "pickups" (shots the director wants to redo), the response is a unanimous "Yes!" Richard Villarino shakes his head in amazement when he recalls audiences who were willing to stay until way after midnight in order to get a scene just right.

Tuesday, August 26, 1986, was a landmark for *Cheers*. "House of Horrors," written by David Angell, was the one hundredth episode filmed. A new set was built that would become Carla's home. "House of Horrors" was one of the rare *Cheers* episodes that took us out of the bar. In it, Carla wants to buy a house, but cannot afford anything she's seen. Cliff knows of one for sale on his mail route, and the price is right. After plunking down her money, Carla finds out why: the house was built over the graveyard of a seventeenth-century prison,

147

where pirates and ne'er-do-wells were interred. Carla is afraid to move in and knows that if her kids find out, they'll be fighting for the rooms where the worst murderers were buried. Cliff offers to stay with her one night to prove there are no ghosts. It's a long but uneventful night, and morning comes—bringing with it a thundering roar and terrifying bright light. It seems the house is also at the end of a runway where planes land when Boston is fogged in. Carla is thrilled. At least the house isn't haunted.

Filming wrapped a little past midnight, and after the audience had left the stage, the cast and crew walked across the lot to stage #10 where the staff and several NBC executives (about 250 people in all) waited to cut the cake marking this special anniversary episode.

Almost every television show has horror stories about network interference, but *Cheers* has had the complete trust of NBC. Warren Littlefield, senior vice-president of series programming, and Tom Posivak, program policy manager, were among some of the loyal network people invited to share in the celebration. Thanks to people like them, a show that premiered with the worst possible ratings was allowed to stay on the air and eventually flourish.

We, the audience, have only one word to offer as a toast to these brilliant men and women, both behind the scenes as well as on camera . . .

CHEERS!

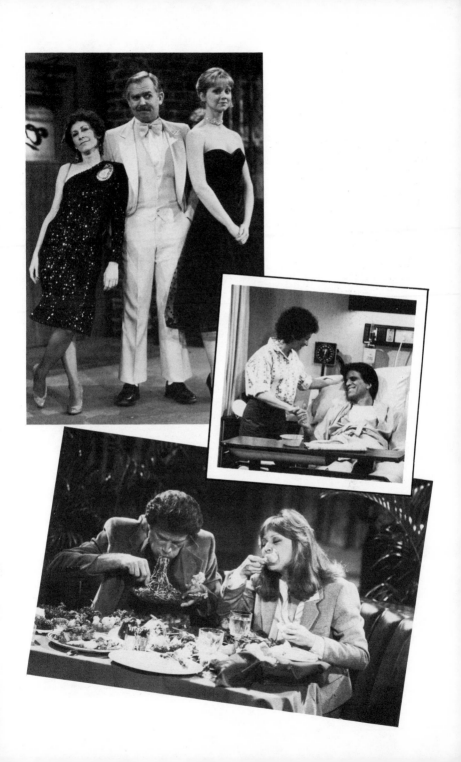

Familiar Faces

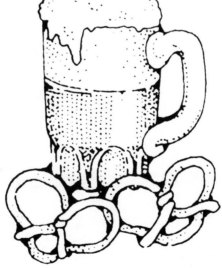

There are a number of semiregulars who round out the population of Cheers.

Alan Koss plays Alan; Tim Cunningham plays Tim; Steve Gianelli plays Steve; Tom Babson plays Tom; Larry Harpel plays Larry; Paul Vaughn plays Paul; Jack Knight plays Jack; and Al Rosen plays the Man Who Said Sinatra.

In addition, recurring characters Nick Tortelli and his wife Loretta are played by Dan Hedaya and Jean Kasem.

Andy, the psychotic murderer, is played by Derek McGrath; Duncan Ross is Boggs, Diane's mother's chauffeur; Michael McGuire plays Sumner Sloan, Diane's ex-fiancé; Fred Dryer plays Dave Richards, sports announcer; and Harry Anderson periodically shows up as Harry—the flimflam man.

Special appearances include Bernadette Birkett (George Wendt's wife) as Tinkerbell in the costume party episode; Playboy bunnies showed up for a charity softball match in which Sam took the competition seriously;

Dick Cavett was featured as himself, as was House Speaker Tip O'Neill, who dropped by for a beer, and Senator Gary Hart stopped in to return Sam's jacket. Diane was stunned to learn Sam and Senator Hart had been Trivial Pursuit partners the night before.

Faces from Other Places

Fred Dryer (*Hunter*) as Dave Richards, sportscaster

Harry Anderson (*Night Court*) as Harry

Rick Dees (KIIS-FM radio DJ) as one of the regulars

Allyce Beasley (*Moonlighting*) as Coach's daughter

Julia Duffy (*Newhart*) as Diane's friend since fourth grade, Rebecca

Barbara Babcock (*Mr. Sunshine*) as Lana, the talent agent

Donna McKechnie (*A Chorus Line*) as Sam's ex-wife, Deborah

Markie Post (*Night Court*) as Heather, Diane's friend who puts the make on Sam

Christopher Lloyd (*Taxi*) as Phillip Semenko, the surrealistic painter

Nancy Marchand (*Lou Grant*) as Hester Crane, Frasier's mother

Carol Kane (*Taxi*) as Amanda, Diane's friend from Golden Brook

Kate Mulgrew (*Mrs. Columbo*) as Councilwoman Janet Eldridge

Max Wright (*Buffalo Bill*) as Jim Fleener, Janet's competition

Gretchen Corbett as Diane's idea of Sam's perfect date

Glynis Johns as Helen Chambers, Diane's mother

Sam Scarber as Lewis, a friend of Cliff's and fellow postman

And
the Winner is...

Awards and Nominations

* Denotes Winner

Emmy Nominations

1982–1983

* Outstanding Comedy Series—*CHEERS*
    (James Burrows, Glen Charles, Les Charles, executive producers; Ken Levine, David Isaacs, co-producers)

  Outstanding Lead Actor in Comedy Series—TED DANSON

* Outstanding Lead Actress in Comedy Series—SHELLEY LONG

  Outstanding Supporting Actor in Comedy Series—NICHOLAS COLASANTO

  Outstanding Supporting Actress in Comedy Series—RHEA PERLMAN

* Outstanding Directing in Comedy Series—JAMES BURROWS ("Showdown—Part II")

* Outstanding Writing in Comedy Series—GLEN CHARLES and LES CHARLES ("Give Me a Ring Sometime")

  Outstanding Writing in Comedy Series—KEN LEVINE, DAVID ISAACS ("The Boys in the Bar")

159

Outstanding Writing in Comedy Series—DAVID LLOYD ("Diane's Perfect Date")

Outstanding Art Direction for a Series—RICHARD SYLBERT, Production Design; GEORGE GAINES, Set Decoration ("Give Me a Ring Sometime")

Outstanding Achievement in Music and Lyrics—GARY PORTNOY, JUDY HART ANGELO (Composer and Lyricist—"Where Everybody Knows Your Name")

Outstanding Film Editing for a Series—ANDREW CHULACK ("Endless Slumper")

* Outstanding Individual Achievement Graphic Design and Title Sequences—JAMES CASTLE, BRUCE BRYANT

1983–1984

* Outstanding Comedy Series—*CHEERS* (Glen Charles, Les Charles, James Burrows, executive producers)

Outstanding Lead Actor in Comedy Series—TED DANSON

Outstanding Lead Actress in Comedy Series—SHELLEY LONG

Outstanding Supporting Actor in Comedy Series— NICHOLAS COLASANTO

Outstanding Supporting Actor in Comedy Series— GEORGE WENDT

* Outstanding Supporting Actress in Comedy Series— RHEA PERLMAN

Outstanding Directing in Comedy Series—JAMES BURROWS ("Old Flames")

* Outstanding Writing in Comedy Series—DAVID ANGELL ("Old Flames")

Outstanding Writing in Comedy Series—GLEN CHARLES and LES CHARLES ("Power May")

Outstanding Writing in Comedy Series—DAVID LLOYD ("The Homicidal Man")

160

* Outstanding Film Editing in Series—ANDREW CHUL-ACK ("Old Flames")

Outstanding Live and Tape Sound Mixing and Sound Effects for a Series—GORDON KLIMUSK, Production; THOMAS HUTH, Postproduction; SAM BLACK, Sound Effects; DOUGLAS GRAY Preproduction ("No Help Wanted")

1984–1985

Outstanding Comedy Series—*CHEERS*
(James Burrows, Glen Charles, Les Charles, executive producers; Ken Estin, Sam Simon, producers)

Outstanding Lead Actor in Comedy Series—TED DANSON

Outstanding Lead Actress in Comedy Series—SHELLEY LONG

Outstanding Supporting Actor in Comedy Series—NICHOLAS COLASANTO

Outstanding Supporting Actor in Comedy Series—JOHN RATZENBERGER

Outstanding Supporting Actor in Comedy Series—GEORGE WENDT

* Outstanding Supporting Actress in Comedy Series—RHEA PERLMAN

Outstanding Directing in Comedy Series—JAMES BURROWS ("Cheerio, Cheers")

Outstanding Writing in Comedy Series—PETER CASEY, DAVID LEE ("I Call Your Name")

Outstanding Writing in Comedy Series—GLEN CHARLES and LES CHARLES ("Rebound Part II")

Outstanding Writing in Comedy Series—DAVID LLOYD ("Sam Turns the Other Cheek")

* Outstanding Live and Tape Sound Mixing and Sound Effects for Series—DOUGLAS GRAY, Preproduction; MICHAEL BALLIN, production; THOMAS HUTH, postproduction; SAM BLACK, Sound Effects ("Executive's Executioner")

161

1985–1986

    Outstanding Comedy Series—*CHEERS*
        (James Burrows, Glen Charles, Les Charles, executive producers; Peter Casey, David Lee, Heide Perlman, David Angell, producers; Tim Berry, co-producer

    Outstanding Lead Actor in Comedy Series—TED DANSON

    Outstanding Lead Actress in Comedy Series—SHELLEY LONG

    Outstanding Supporting Actor in Comedy Series—JOHN RATZENBERGER

    Outstanding Supporting Actor in Comedy Series—GEORGE WENDT

* Outstanding Supporting Actress in Comedy Series—RHEA PERLMAN

    Outstanding Directing in Comedy Series—JAMES BURROWS ("The Triangle")

    Outstanding Writing in Comedy Series—PETER CASEY, DAVID LEE ("2 Good 2 Be 4 Real")

    Outstanding Film Editing for Series—ANDY ACKERMAN ("Birth, Death, Love & Rice")

    Outstanding Film Editing for Series—DOUGLAS HINES, A.C.E. ("The Triangle")

* Outstanding Sound Mixing for Comedy Series—MICHAEL BALLIN, ROBERT DOUGLAS, DOUGLAS GRAY, THOMAS HUTH ("Fear Is My Copilot")

Additional Awards:

1983, Golden Globe—(Best Actress in a Comedy Series) SHELLEY LONG

1983, People's Choice—(Favorite Television Program) *CHEERS*

1983, Television Critics Association—(Best New Series) *CHEERS*

162

1983, Alliance for Gay Artists Award—"The Boys in the Bar"

1984, Directors Guild of America—JAMES BURROWS ("Showdown II")

1984, Writers Guild of America—GLEN CHARLES and LES CHARLES ("Give Me a Ring Sometime")

1984, Writers Guild of America—KEN LEVINE and DAVID ISAACS ("The Boys in the Bar")

1985, Golden Globe—(Best Actress in a Comedy Series) SHELLEY LONG

1985, Writers Guild of America—MICHAEL J. WEITHORN ("Sumner's Return")

1985, Chicago International Film Festival: Silver Hugo—"Cheerio, Cheers" episode

The Cheers Log

(*Cheers* episodes aired out of sequence; in order to accurately follow the story line of the first four seasons, episodes are listed chronologically by air date.)

First Season: 1982–1983

Starring: Ted Danson, Shelley Long, Nicholas Colasanto, Rhea Perlman, John Ratzenberger, and George Wendt

"GIVE ME A RING SOMETIME"   (#001)
                                        AIR DATE: 9/30/82
Diane and her fiancé, Sumner Sloan, stop by Cheers on the way to their honeymoon. When Sumner goes to retrieve his grandmother's wedding ring from his ex-wife, he promptly falls back in love with her. A very uncomfortable Diane is suddenly stranded in a bar with no money, no job, no future. Sam thinks working at Cheers would be good for her, and she ultimately accepts his offer, having nowhere else to turn.

Written by: Glen Charles and Les Charles
Directed by: James Burrows
Guest Cast: Michael McGuire as Sumner Sloan; Margaret Wheeler as Mrs. Littlefield; Ron Frazier as Ron; Bill Wiley as the Customer; John P. Navin as the Boy; Elsa Ravan as the Nurse

"SAM'S WOMEN"   (#002) AIR DATE: 10/7/82
Sam has always been happy with airheads, and now, thanks to Diane, he is depressed because he thinks an intelligent woman would never fall for his lines. When he pays Diane an eloquent compliment, she is stunned and flattered until Sam admits it was a dumb idea. She saw right through it. Diane realizes she's been had and Sam figures it's back to bimbos.
Written by: Earl Pomerantz
Directed by: James Burrows
Guest Cast: Angela Aames as Brandee; Donna McKechnie as Debra; Jack Knight as Jack; Donnelly Rhodes as Leo Metz

"THE TORTELLI TORT"   (#004) AIR DATE: 10/14/82
Carla beats up an obnoxious Yankee fan, Ed, who starts berating the Red Sox. Ed threatens to sue Sam if the obstreperous waitress isn't fired. Carla agrees to enter therapy, and when Ed returns he says if she can hold her tongue, she can stay. Carla remains magnificently calm as he hurls a string of insults her way. Sam now warns him not to keep knocking the Bruins. Why? He points to two suspended players who offer to "escort" Ed to his car.
Written by: Tom Reeder
Directed by: James Burrows
Guest Cast: Ron Karabatsos as Ed; John Fiedler as Fred; Stephen Keep as Dr. Gordon

"SAM AT ELEVEN"   (#005) AIR DATE: 10/21/82
Sam is excited about being interviewed by Dave Rich-

ards, a famous sportscaster. Malone doesn't know he was the station's last choice until mid-interview when he's abruptly replaced by a junior-high gymnast. When Diane attempts to console him, Sam takes advantage of her kindness. Her reflex is to judo-flip him onto the pool table, then sincerely ask if he would tell her the end of his story.

Written by: Glen Charles and Les Charles
Directed by: James Burrows
Guest Cast: Fred Dryer as Dave Richards; Harry Anderson as Harry; Rick Dees as a Young Guy; Julie Brown as Cathy

"ANY FRIEND   (#008) AIR DATE: 11/4/82
OF DIANE'S"

After a ruined romance with an intellectual, Diane's prim friend Rebecca wants a fling with someone earthy. Diane still hasn't come to grips with her feelings for Sam, and to her horror she realizes Rebecca has set her sights on him.

Written by: Ken Levine and David Isaacs
Directed by: James Burrows
Guest Cast: Julia Duffy as Rebecca; Macon McCalman as Darrell

"FRIENDS, ROMANS,   (#013) AIR DATE: 11/11/82
ACCOUNTANTS"

As coordinator of his company's annual bash, Norm has chosen a "toga party" theme. It could mean a promotion if it's a hit. The big night arrives and Norm is the only one dressed in a sheet. Even worse, the date he got for his boss "fell off her shoes." Norm asks Diane to fill in. The boss is young and handsome and Diane is happy to help until he turns out to be a letch, and Norm, protecting Diane's virtue, is promptly fired.

Written by: Ken Levine and David Isaacs
Directed by: James Burrows
Guest Cast: James Read as H. W. Sawyer

"TRUCE OR CONSEQUENCES"

(#006) AIR DATE: 11/18/82

If Diane and Carla don't stop fighting, one of them will have to go. Carla offers friendship in the form of a secret—her son Gino is really Sam's—and the next day Diane can't keep her mouth shut. Carla knew this would happen so she told her the biggest lie she could.

Written by: Ken Levine and David Isaacs
Directed by: James Burrows
Guest Cast: Jack Knight as Jack; Peter Van Norden as the Cymbals Player

"COACH RETURNS TO ACTION"

(#010) AIR DATE: 11/25/82

Coach is infatuated with Nina, a young woman who's moving into his building, but he's too shy to ask her out. She stops by Cheers, and Sam, ignoring Diane's protests, asks her out, but Nina's not interested in Sam. Diane insists Coach try to get her attention. Coach does—the only way he knows how—by falling down the stairs: a sympathy ploy that works every time.

Written by: Earl Pomerantz
Directed by: James Burrows
Guest Cast: Murphy Cross as Nina Bradshaw

"ENDLESS SLUMPER"

(#009) AIR DATE: 12/2/82

Sam gives his good-luck charm to a Sox relief pitcher who's in a slump. Two weeks later, Sam's life has completely fallen apart. Diane didn't know he was so superstitious. Sam finally admits it was the bottle cap from the last drink he ever had. It was his "rock" when things got tough. Sam opens a beer, and Diane panics until he looks at the cap, pockets it, and pours out the beer.

Written by: Sam Simon
Directed by: James Burrows
Guest Cast: Christopher McDonald as Rick Walker; Anne

170

Haney as Miss Guilder; Bobby Shafran as Bobby; David Kellman as David; Eddy S. Galland as Eddy

"ONE FOR THE BOOK" (#003) AIR DATE: 12/9/82
It's a busy night: A World War I veteran, Buzz, is waiting for his old brigade to show up for a reunion; a young man is having his last night on the town before joining a monastery; and Diane is busy writing down "snippets" of interesting dialogue she hears around the bar. By evening's end, none of Buzz's comrades has shown; Kevin is convinced he's made the right choice; and a frustrated Sam is the only one who hasn't said something worthy of Diane's little book.
Written by: Katherine Green
Directed by: James Burrows
Guest Cast: Ian Wolfe as Buzz Crowder; Boyd Bodwell as Kevin; Jack Knight as Jack

"THE SPY WHO CAME (#012) AIR DATE: 12/16/82
IN FOR A COLD ONE"
Carla suspects that a customer is an international spy. Diane knows he's a liar, but Sam explains that people can be anyone they want in a bar. The man admits Diane was right. He's old and lonely, but has written some poetry. Diane tries to find him a publisher, then realizes he's lied again. When he explains he's really rich and just looking for friends to leave his money to, they all toss him out thinking he's fibbing again—just as his driver arrives to announce that his limo is waiting.
Written by: David Lloyd
Directed by: James Burrows
Guest Cast: Ellis Rabb as Eric Finch; Jack Knight as Jack

"NOW PITCHING: (#016) AIR DATE: 1/6/83
SAM MALONE"
Lana, a talent agent, makes Sam the new star of a local TV commercial. Sam is very down: he's been sleeping

with Lana and wants to break it off, but can't. Diane encourages him to try. Lana dangles a national commercial under his nose, but when Sam finally makes his point, she dumps him. Late at night, Sam wistfully watches his commercial on TV. He was good.
Written by: Ken Levine and David Isaacs
Directed by: James Burrows
Guest Cast: Barbara Babcock as Lana Marshall; Rick Hill as Tibor Svetkovic; Paul Vaughn as Paul; Luis Tiant as himself

"LET ME COUNT   (#011) AIR DATE: 1/13/83
THE WAYS"
Diane learns that her cat, Elizabeth Barrett Browning, has died. Everyone in the bar is more interested in a Celtics game than her grief. Finally, she pulls Sam into the back room. All she wants is a little compassion. Sam apologizes and hugs her tightly. It's nice . . . until Sam gets too friendly and another brief fight ensues. No more hugging, but Sam is genuinely sorry about her cat.
Written by: Heide Perlman
Directed by: James Burrows
Guest Cast: Mark King as Marshall Lipton; Jack Knight as Jack

"FATHER KNOWS LAST"   (#014) AIR DATE: 1/20/83
Carla is five months pregnant and finally confesses that the father is Marshall Lipton, the nerdy Ph.D. from MIT. Marshall wants to marry Carla. Diane learns that Carla is using him—the real father is Carla's ex-husband, Nick. At Diane's prodding, Carla tells Marshall the truth. He is destroyed, but Sam tells him if he really loves Carla, marry her anyway. Carla is overcome. This is the first man who ever said, "I love you."
Written by: Heide Perlman
Directed by: James Burrows
Guest Cast: Mark King as Marshall Lipton; Bernard Behrens as Justice of the Peace

172

"THE BOYS IN THE BAR" (#015) AIR DATE: 1/27/83
Sam's old roommate, Tom, has written *Behind the Mask*, a book about his coming out of the closet, and is "promoting" it at Cheers. When a photo of Sam and Tom together appears in the paper, everyone thinks Cheers will become a gay bar. Sam sticks to his guns while the regulars make fools of themselves trying to identify possible gays in the bar.
Written by: Ken Levine and David Isaacs
Directed by: James Burrows
Guest Cast: Alan Autry as Tom Jackson; Jack Knight as Jack; Lee Ryan as Bob; Kenneth Tigar as Fred; John Furey as Larry; Michael Kerns as Richard; Rick Dees as Rick; Julie Brown as Cathy; Paul Vaughn as Paul

"DIANE'S PERFECT DATE" (#017) AIR DATE: 2/10/83
Both Sam and Diane are convinced they could find the perfect date for the other. From Diane's description, Sam is sure she's talking about herself, and he feels he's right for her. When Diane shows up with Gretchen, Sam grabs a stranger to be Diane's date. To Diane's horror, Andy turns out to be a paroled murderer. By evening's end, Sam and Diane still won't admit to any real feelings for each other.
Written by: David Lloyd
Directed by: James Burrows
Guest Cast: Gretchen Corbett as Gretchen; Derek McGrath as Andy; Douglas Sheehan as Walter Franklin

"NO CONTEST" (#019) AIR DATE: 2/17/83
Sam has entered Diane in the Annual Miss Boston Barmaid contest. Diane wants out until she realizes this could be the perfect forum to speak out against these dehumanizing contests. She gives an impassioned speech on survival to the judges—and wins. When her prize—a trip to Bermuda—is announced, she sells out and squeals with joy. Later, Sam consoles her, congratulating her on being spontaneous for the first time in her life.

173

Written by: Heide Perlman
Directed by: James Burrows
Guest Cast: Tip O'Neill as himself; Renee Gentry as Yvonne; Tessa Richarde as Bonnie; Sharon Peters as Jocelyn; Paul Vaughn as Paul; Daryl Roach as Judge #1; Bob Ari as Judge #2; James Sherwood as Judge #3; Charlie Stavola as Emcee

"PICK A CON . . .   (#018) AIR DATE: 2/24/83
ANY CON"
Sam discovers that Coach's gin-rummy partner, George—a con-man out of Vegas—has fleeced Coach out of $8,000. Sam sets up a sting with Harry, the local flimflam man, to get the money back. The big game, and Harry is losing—with winning hands! It looks like Sam's been had until Harry does win all their money back.
Written by: David Angell
Directed by: James Burrows
Guest Cast: Harry Anderson as Harry; Reid Shelton as George Wheeler

"SOMEONE SINGLE,   (#020) AIR DATE: 3/3/83
SOMEONE BLUE"
When "Mummy" comes to visit, Diane learns of a little stipulation in her father's will: her mother's money will be cut off if Diane isn't married by tomorrow. Diane is forced to propose to Sam, who good-naturedly agrees. It almost happens. Mid-ceremony, Diane catches Sam leering at a pretty girl in the bar. The wedding is stopped. The family chauffeur volunteers to marry her mother; he's been embezzling for years and is quite comfortable.
Written by: David Angell
Directed by: James Burrows
Guest Cast: Glynis Johns as Helen Chambers; Duncan Ross as Boggs; Dean Dittman as Harrison Fiedler

"COACH'S DAUGHTER"   (#007) AIR DATE: 3/10/83
Lisa, Coach's daughter, comes to Cheers to introduce her fiancé, Roy, to her dad. Roy is an obnoxious lout, and Coach doesn't understand why she's marrying him. Lisa gently tries to explain that she's not very pretty and this may be her only chance to get married. Coach finally convinces her she's beautiful and doesn't have to settle for less.
Written by: Ken Estin
Directed by: James Burrows
Guest Cast: Allyce Beasley as Lisa; Philip Charles Mac-Kenzie as Roy; Tim Cunningham as Chuck

"SHOWDOWN—PART I"   (#021) AIR DATE: 3/24/83
Sam's successful brother, Derek, comes by for a visit. Everyone is taken with him, and Sam's feelings of inadequacy grow. When Diane becomes smitten as well, Sam is desolate. Derek has asked Diane to go away for the weekend, and she wants Sam to say anything so she has a reason to stay. Neither will verbalize the way he feels, and Diane must leave with Derek.
Written by: Glen Charles and Les Charles
Directed by: James Burrows
Guest Cast: George Ball as Derek (we never *see* Derek); Alan Koss as Alan; Paul Vaughn as Paul; Deborah Shelton as Debbie

"SHOWDOWN—PART II"   (#022) AIR DATE: 3/31/83
Diane has been dating Sam's brother, Derek, who's asked her to come to Paris. Diane admits to Coach how much she likes Sam and wishes he'd do something to stop her from leaving. She goes into Sam's office, but he says nothing. She finally tells him how she feels and gets him to admit he cares for her. In an attempt to seal this with a kiss, they get into another fight because Diane won't stop talking about it. The fight gets hotter and heavier, with the pair very "turned on."

175

Written by: Glen Charles and Les Charles
Directed by: James Burrows
Guest Cast: Tim Cunningham as Chuck; Alan Koss as Alan; Paul Vaughn as Paul; Helen Page Camp as Helen; Peggy Kubena as Cindy

Second Season: 1983—1984

Starring: Ted Danson, Shelley Long, Nicholas Colasanto, Rhea Perlman, John Ratzenberger, and George Wendt

"POWER PLAY"   (#023) AIR DATE: 9/29/83
The second season opens right where last year left off. Diane and Sam decide to consummate their relationship at Diane's apartment. It almost happens, until Diane's stuffed animals cause another fight and Sam is thrown out. Deciding to be more macho, he storms back and breaks down her door. He'll show her who's boss. Once again, the animals get in the way and, in frustration, Sam flings them out the window. This time the fight is knock-down and dirty. When they are both spent, Diane admits she just didn't want him to think she was easy.
Written by: Glen Charles and Les Charles
Directed by: James Burrows
Guest Cast: Alan Koss as Alan; Paul Vaughn as Paul

"LIL SISTER DONTCHA"   (#025) AIR DATE: 10/13/83
Carla's "good" sister, Annette, is filling in while Carla has her baby. She's sweet, innocent, and making a lot of dates around the bar. Sam thinks she's just naive until Annette goes after him, too. Meanwhile, Cliff has asked her out. She said yes and Cliff's in love. It's up to Norm to tell his best friend what kind of girl Annette really is.
Written by: Heide Perlman

Directed by: James Burrows
Guest Cast: Rhea Perlman as Annette Lozupone; Paul Vaughn as Paul

"PERSONAL BUSINESS"   (#027) AIR DATE: 10/20/83
Norm has been thrown out of his house and is now sleeping in Sam's office at Cheers. Meanwhile, because Sam is sleeping with Diane, Carla feels he's playing favorites when it comes to the workload. Diane, wanting to avoid another fight, quits. She finally finds another job, and learns her new boss wants only her body. When Sam offers her her old job back, Diane is only too happy to accept.
Written by: Tom Reeder
Directed by: James Burrows

"THE HOMICIDAL HAM"   (#024) AIR DATE: 10/27/83
Andy, the murderer, wants to go back to jail. Diane learns he's interested in acting and offers to do a scene with him for a drama-professor friend. They choose the murder scene from *Othello,* and when Andy catches her kissing Sam right before show time, the scene is played out for real. Sam isn't about to interrupt Shakespeare and Diane is almost strangled before anyone realizes what's happening.
Written by: David Lloyd
Directed by: James Burrows
Guest Cast: Derek McGrath as Andy Schroeder; Paul Vaughn as Paul; Alan Koss as Alan; Drew Snyder as Phil; Severn Darden as Professor deWitt

"SUMNER'S RETURN"   (#028) AIR DATE: 11/3/83
Sumner, Diane's ex, shows up wanting Diane and a date to join him and his wife, Barbara, for dinner—no hard feelings. Sam knows he embarrasses Diane and, at Cliff's suggestion, reads *War and Peace* before the big night. Barbara never shows. Sam is out of his element

and certain that Sumner wants Diane back. Diane isn't interested. Sam read that long book for her. The only thing better would be to see the movie together. *Movie?* Cliff never said it was made into a movie!
Written by: Michael J. Weithorn
Directed by: James Burrows
Guest Cast: Michael McGuire as Sumner Sloan

"AFFAIRS OF THE HEART" (#029) AIR DATE: 11/10/83
Carla's very skeptical about a nice man who hits on her. He's got to have a flaw, but try as she might she can't find one. Certain it must be a shortcoming in the bedroom, she borrows Diane's apartment to find out. Coach tells Diane the guy said he had a heart condition and Sam and Diane rush to save Carla. It's too late. The deed is done, and the man is fine. Carla is disgusted to learn he chose her because she didn't excite him too much. Only thing worse—she was in Diane's bed.
Written by: Heide Perlman
Directed by: James Burrows
Guest Cast: Dan Amendolia as Hank Sweeney; Paul Willson as Art

"OLD FLAMES" (#032) AIR DATE: 11/17/83
When Dave Richards drops by and learns Sam and Diane are an item, he bets they can't go twenty-four hours without fighting. To hedge his bet, Dave shows up with two dates and leaves one for Sam to take home. Next day, Sam can't wait to tell Diane that he had the chance and didn't do anything. Diane's furious it went even that far until she hears him tell Dave how much he cares for her.
Written by: David Angell
Directed by: James Burrows
Guest Cast: Fred Dryer as Dave Richards; Elizabeth McIvor as Didi

178

"MANAGER COACH"   (#026) AIR DATE: 11/24/83
When Coach takes over the management of a Little
League team, he suddenly turns into a tyrant. The kids
threaten mutiny, and Coach discovers he's turning into
Mr. Spires—a teacher he's hated all his life. He doesn't
want these kids to feel that way about him. He was just
trying to do what he felt was right. He realizes in time
that it's okay to win and have fun, too.
Written by: Earl Pomerantz
Directed by: James Burrows
Guest Cast: Paul Vaughn as Paul; Alan Koss as Alan;
Herb Mitchell as Mr. Sherwin; Martin Davis as Tank;
Elliot Scott as PeeWee

"THEY CALLED ME   (#031) AIR DATE: 12/1/83
MAYDAY"
Norm is still sleeping in Sam's office, and his old school
buddy, Wally, is making moves on wife Vera. Talkshow
host Dick Cavett drops by and suggests Sam's life story
would make an interesting book. Diane helps Sam write
a sample chapter, but Cavett tells them it's not sexy
enough to sell. Diane won't prostitute her talent writing
smut books, but under a pseudonym . . . she and Sam
rush into his office to spice up the manuscript.
Written by: David Angell
Directed by: James Burrows
Guest Cast: Dick Cavett as himself; Walter Olkewicz as
Wally

"HOW DO I LOVE THEE . . .(#033) AIR DATE: 12/8/83
LET ME CALL YOU BACK"
Diane buys Sam tickets for the Hagler fight. He hugs
her, saying, "I love you." Diane presses him on this,
and he explains he says that to all his friends. She
suggests he think about their relationship, and when
time's up, he has no idea why they're together. She

179

admits neither does she. He starts to say "I love you" again, and can't. Diane is thrilled. That means he means it.

Written by: Earl Pomerantz
Directed by: James Burrows
Guest Cast: Harry Anderson as Harry; Alan Koss as Alan

"JUST THREE FRIENDS"   (#037) AIR DATE: 12/15/83
While a vicious guard dog that Coach purchased is locked in Sam's office, Diane is hoping she, Sam, and her best pal, Heather, can all become good friends. Sam likes the idea of a friendship with a beautiful woman, but is positive Heather is coming on to him. Dinner for three is a disaster. Diane's jealousy grows as she watches Heather flirt with Sam. Sam pleads innocent, and they all hug, Diane hugging Sam so he can't hug Heather.

Written by: David Lloyd
Directed by: James Burrows
Guest Cast: Markie Post as Heather Landon

"WHERE THERE'S A   (#030) AIR DATE: 12/22/83
WILL . . ."
A dying man comes into Cheers and leaves $10,000 for his new friends at the bar. It's Sam's responsibility to disburse the money. Things turn ugly as everyone fights for the lion's share of the money. Sam hates this and burns the will, then tells Diane he burned a fake. *He's* keeping it all. Diane convinces him it's wrong, and Sam performs another sleight of hand only to discover this time he accidentally burned the real will.

Written by: Nick Arnold
Directed by: James Burrows
Guest Cast: George Gaynes as Malcolm Kramer; Alan Koss as Alan; Tom Babson as Tom

"BATTLE OF THE EXES"   (#034) AIR DATE: 1/5/84
Carla receives a wedding invitation from her ex-husband,

Nick; he's getting remarried. She won't go to the wedding without a date and asks Sam to escort her. When Nick sees her with Sam, he thinks Carla was fooling around with Sam while they were still married. Now Nick wants her back, but Carla knows it's just jealousy talking. Sam gives her a "pity" kiss and she tells him she's had better. Sam says he hasn't. Carla knows.
Written by: Ken Estin and Sam Simon
Directed by: James Burrows
Guest Cast: Dan Hedaya as Nick; Jean Kasem as Loretta

"NO HELP WANTED"   (#036) AIR DATE: 1/12/84
Norm's unemployment has run out and Diane talks Sam into hiring him as the Cheers' accountant. When Norm learns Sam has had his regular accountant also do his tax returns, he is insulted and threatens to leave Cheers forever. Fine, if he can't separate business from friendship, Sam says, "Go." Norm then pulls Sam into Sam's office and privately begs him to let him stay.
Written by: Max Tash
Directed by: James Burrows

"COACHIE MAKES THREE" (#035) AIR DATE: 1/19/84
Coach keeps tagging along on dates with Sam and Diane. Finally, they get him a date with a bank teller, Katherine, whom he likes. The evening is a success, but Coach is still hanging around. They finally tell him outright they'd like to be alone, then feel terrible. When they try to invite him back, he says he's got plans. Their guilt mounts until they learn he *is* going away with Katherine for the weekend.
Written by: Heide Perlman
Directed by: James Burrows
Guest Cast: Eve Roberts as Katherine

"CLIFF'S ROCKY MOMENT"(#040) AIR DATE: 1/26/84
Even though Diane has won the football pool, Sam tries

to show her the "proper" way to pick winners. Meanwhile, a customer picks a fight with Cliff because he won't shut up, but Cliff won't fight. He tells everyone he's a black belt and could kill him. No one believes him. He brings in a board, and, barefoot, kicks it in half. Everyone wants to buy him a drink, but first he needs Diane to take him to a doctor. He doesn't know anything about karate.

Written by: David Lloyd
Directed by: James Burrows
Guest Cast: Peter Iacangelo as Vic; Sam Scarber as Lewis

"FORTUNE AND MEN'S WEIGHTS"   (#039) AIR DATE: 2/2/84

Carla is very superstitious about the new "Weight and Your Fortune" machine Coach bought. Everyone's fortunes are coming true. Diane's deals with deceit in romance and she admits to Sam she went to a concert with another man. Sam blows her confession out of proportion and kicks the machine. Another fortune card pops out. Diane will believe anything it says. She looks. "All Out—Order More Today." She feels that's a good sign, and she and Sam are back together.

Written by: Heide Perlman
Directed by: James Burrows

"SNOW JOB"   (#038) AIR DATE 2/9/84

Norm has made a new friend and begins ignoring Cliff. Diane, meanwhile, is confident that Sam won't take his annual ski trip with the boys. Three times Sam tries to get away, and each time Diane instills enough guilt to make him turn back. Ultimately Sam doesn't go, and Norm realizes Cliff is the best friend he has.

Written by: David Angell
Directed by: James Burrows
Guest Cast: Will Nye as George Foley

"COACH BURIES A   (#041) AIR DATE: 2/16/84
GRUDGE"
Coach's old pal and teammate, T-Bone Scarpigeone, has
passed away and Diane suggests they have a memorial
at Cheers. Coach is pleased until he overhears Sam tell
Diane that T-Bone once hit on Angela, Coach's wife.
Now Coach hates T-Bone, and Angela, too, for never
telling him. Diane convinces him to forgive them both.
He gives a beautiful eulogy, then learns from the guys
that T-Bone hit on everyone's wife.
Written by: David Lloyd
Directed by: James Burrows
Guest Cast: Al Rosen as Al

"NORMAN'S CONQUEST"   (#042) AIR DATE: 2/23/84
Norm's new client, Emily, makes a play for him, and
Norm is embarrassed to tell the guys he didn't follow
through with it. Sam convinces him to tell the others the
truth, but when they start calling him "wuss," Norm is
back to his old habit of razzing Vera, only now we really
know how much he loves her.
Written by: Lissa Levin
Directed by: James Burrows
Guest Cast: Anne Schedeen as Emily Phillips; Alan Koss
as Alan; Tim Cunningham as Tim; Steve Giannelli as Steve

"I'LL BE SEEING YOU"   (#043) AIR DATE: 5/3/84
—PART I
Sam wants to give Diane a portrait of herself, and Cliff
says he knows an artist on his mail route. Phillip Semenko
is a surrealistic painter and is insulted by Sam's request.
When Diane enters, however, he becomes enraptured
by her face and must paint her.

"I'LL BE SEEING YOU"   (#044) AIR DATE: 5/10/84
—PART II
Diane has been posing for Semenko. He keeps making

183

insulting remarks about Sam and finally puts his brush down. He knows Sam won't appreciate the picture; Diane says he will. When Sam finds out that Diane is posing for Semenko, another fight starts. This one is the big one and Diane walks out for good. Sam is left alone with the still-wrapped portrait. Alone, he unveils it, and with no one to see, looks and says appreciatively, "Wow."
Written by: Glen Charles and Les Charles
Directed by: James Burrows
Guest Cast: Christopher Lloyd as Phillip Semenko; Steve Giannelli as Steve

Third Season: 1984—1985

Starring: Ted Danson, Shelley Long, Nicholas Colasanto, Rhea Perlman, John Ratzenberger, George Wendt, and Kelsey Grammer

"REBOUND—PART I"   (#045) AIR DATE: 9/27/84
In the aftermath of their explosive separation, Sam has started drinking again and returned to his playboy ways. Diane has just come back from a self-imposed stay at the Golden Brook Sanitarium. Coach, concerned about Sam's drinking, asks Diane to talk to him. She suggests he get help from her doctor, Frasier Crane, but fails to tell Sam she and Frasier are now lovers.
Written by: Glen Charles and Les Charles
Directed by: James Burrows
Guest Cast: Duncan Ross as Boggs

"REBOUND—PART II"   (#046) AIR DATE: 10/4/84
Frasier has helped Sam stop drinking, and Diane feels it's time to tell Sam about her and Frasier. When another waitress quits, Sam asks Diane to come back. She doesn't want to, but Coach tell her that if she leaves, Sam will

go back to drinking. Convinced she can work with him without it affecting her romance with Frasier, she agrees. When Frasier suggests she and Sam kiss and make up, the old feelings are off and running again.
Written by: Glen Charles and Les Charles
Directed by: James Burrows
Guest Cast: Duncan Ross as Boggs; P. J. Soles as Julie; Al Rosen as the Man Who Said Sinatra

"I CALL YOUR NAME"   (#051) AIR DATE: 10/18/84
Cliff is scared stiff because he turned in a fellow postman for stealing and the big guy is looking for him. At the same time, Sam deduces from talking to Frasier that Diane calls out his name in intimate moments. Sam can't stop gloating, and Diane is furious. She makes a play for Sam, then when least expected (or wanted) calls out Frasier's name.
Written by: Peter Casey and David Lee
Directed by: James Burrows
Guest Cast: Sam Scarber as Lewis

"FAIRY TALES CAN   (#056) AIR DATE: 10/25/84
COME TRUE"
Cheers has a costume party for Halloween, and Cliff meets the woman of his dreams, but is nervous about their first date without masks. Meanwhile, Frasier has asked Sam to take Diane to a concert, and both she and Sam are nervous about their upcoming date.
Written by: Sam Simon
Directed by: James Burrows
Guest Cast: Bernadette Birkett (George Wendt's real-life wife) as Tinkerbell

"SAM TURNS THE OTHER   (#048) AIR DATE: 11/1/84
CHEEK"
Sam unknowingly breaks his rule of never dating married women. When the husband comes gunning for

185

him, Sam talks him out of the gun, but it accidentally fires when Sam puts it in his back pocket. He makes up a story about thwarting a holdup, but Diane suspects his actions were less heroic. When the husband returns, angry at the publicity Sam is getting, Diane is the one who saves Sam, but makes him promise he'll tell the truth to the guys.

Written by: David Lloyd
Directed by: James Burrows
Guest Cast: Kim Lankford as Maxine; Carmen Argenziano as Marvin

"COACH IN LOVE—PART I"(#049) AIR DATE: 11/8/84
An attractive older woman, Irene, and her daughter come into Cheers and it's love at first sight for Coach. She feels the same way, and after two weeks of dating, Coach asks her to marry him. Sam, meanwhile, is getting nowhere in his effort to date the pretty young daughter. Part I ends with Irene saying yes, then receiving a call from her daughter. Irene just won a $2-million lottery and suddenly has forgotten all about Coach.

"COACH IN LOVE—PART II"(#050) AIR DATE: 11/15/84
Irene has postponed the wedding three times, but Coach hasn't given up hope. Irene tries to explain that the money has changed her, but Coach doesn't believe it and hangs on right up until the wedding hour. She never shows, but when the phone rings, Coach knows it's her and gives her a touching farewell speech.

Written by: David Angell
Directed by: James Burrows
Guest Cast: Bette Ford as Irene Blanchard; Ellen Regan as Sue Blanchard

"DIANE MEETS MOM"   (#052) AIR DATE: 11/22/84
Diane's first meeting with Frasier's mom is lovely until Mom threatens to kill her if she doesn't leave Frasier

alone. Sam convinces Diane that Mom was kidding. When Diane tries the same "humor" on her, Frasier is horrified. Diane convinces Mom she's the best thing that ever happened to Frasier. Mom, however, asks Sam what it would take to get Sam to go out with Diane again. Sam says there isn't enough money in the world.
Written by: David Lloyd
Directed by: James Burrows
Guest Cast: Nancy Marchand as Hester Crane; Larry Harpel as Larry

"AN AMERICAN FAMILY" (#047) AIR DATE: 11/29/84
Carla's ex-husband, Nick, comes by with his new bride, Loretta, to take one of Nick's kids to live with them. As much as Carla complains about the kids, she doesn't want to lose one, and the entire bar helps her get her boy back. Meanwhile, Sam is trying desperately to get away for a ski weekend, but each time he tries, Diane makes him feel so guilty that he can't go and have a good time.
Written by: Heide Perlman
Directed by: James Burrows
Guest Cast: Dan Hedaya as Nick; Jean Kasem as Loretta; Tom Babson as Tom

"DIANE'S ALLERGY" (#055) AIR DATE: 12/6/84
Diane moves in with Frasier and develops an allergy to his dog. Sam takes the dog, but Diane's allergy gets worse. Sam delights in watching Diane and Frasier convince each other everything's fine. Ultimately, they decide things are moving too fast, and Diane moves out. Meanwhile, it's Carla's birthday, and all she is getting are gag gifts—even crystal dribble glasses from Frasier and Diane.
Written by: David Lloyd
Directed by: James Burrows

"PETERSON CRUSOE"   (#054) AIR DATE: 12/13/84
When Norm learns the spot on his X ray wasn't serious, he takes another look at his life. He decides to chuck it all and live in a hut on Bora Bora. The guys get letters from him; it all sounds like the ideal life until Sam discovers Norm hiding in his office. Sam lets the cat out of the bag, and everyone tries to convince Norm it's okay to come out; they understand about dreams that go awry.
Written by: David Angell
Directed by: James Burrows

"A DITCH IN TIME"   (#053) AIR DATE: 12/20/84
Sam flirts with a pretty customer, Amanda, and takes Diane's warnings as jealousy talking until he finds out Amanda was with Diane in the sanitarium. Her problem: compulsive affairs that end in suicide attempts if she's rejected. Sam can't get out of it, and only when Diane tells Amanda that Sam was "Ralph" in her group therapy sessions does Amanda run for her life.
Written by: Ken Estin
Directed by: James Burrows
Guest Cast: Carol Kane as Amanda; Larry Harpel as Larry

"WHODUNIT"   (#057) AIR DATE: 1/3/85
Frasier's mentor, Dr. Bennett Ludlow, visits Cheers and is immediately taken with Carla. Frasier and Diane are stunned and speechless, while Carla and Bennett have a whirlwind romance. Carla discovers she's pregnant with Bennett's child and he wants to marry her. Carla must turn him down gently.
Written by: Tom Reeder
Directed by: James Burrows
Guest Cast: James Karen as Dr. Bennett Ludlow

"THE HEART IS A LONELY (#058) AIR DATE: 1/10/85 SNIPEHUNTER"

The regulars agree to take a depressed Frasier on their fishing trip. They return, having sent Frasier on a snipe hunt in the snow. Diane is horrified. When Frasier shows up, he is thrilled at being one of the guys. He's ready to go back to the woods to find that snipe. The guys feel guilty and say they'll help. To Diane's delight, Frasier plans to leave them up there while he sneaks back.

Written by: Heide Perlman
Directed by: James Burrows
Guest Cast: Tim Cunningham as Tim; Alan Koss as Alan

"KING OF THE HILL"   (#061) AIR DATE: 1/24/85

Diane is all for Sam's playing on a charity softball team, until she learns it's the Playboy Bunny team. The guys are all behind Sammy, but the day of the game Sam turns competitive and everyone's mad because they didn't get to see the little cottontails running around the bases.

Written by: Elliot Shoenman
Directed by: James Burrows
Guest Cast: Steve Giannelli as Steve; John Hancock as Lenny; Playboy Playmates: Geana Tomasina, Hedie Sorenson, Ola Ray; David Paymer as Reporter; Larry Harpel as Larry

"TEACHER'S PET"   (#062) AIR DATE: 1/31/85

Sam returns to school to get his diploma, and Coach decides to join him. Both are star pupils, but Diane learns that Coach is studying and Sam is engaging in extracurricular activities with the teacher. Diane urges Sam to get his degree honestly, which he does, and also discovers he now knows more state capitals than Diane.

Written by: Tom Reeder
Directed by: James Burrows
Guest Cast: Steve Giannelli as Steve; Larry Harpel as Larry

"THE MAIL GOES TO JAIL" (#064) AIR DATE: 2/7/85
Cliff is suffering from a bad cold and Norm offers to
finish his mail route. When Cliff learns Norm was arrested for tampering with the mail, he's afraid he'll lose
his job if he tells his superiors the truth. Ultimately,
friendship is more important than his career, and he
confesses. Norm is free and Cliff learns he didn't lose
his job.
Written by: David Lloyd
Directed by: James Burrows
Guest Cast: Larry Harpel as Larry; Al Rosen as the Man
Who Said Sinatra

"BEHIND EVERY (#066) AIR DATE: 2/21/85
GREAT MAN"
Sam is hot for Paula, a tough reporter doing a story on
the Boston singles scene. She's turned off by Sam, and
as he tries to impress her with his knowledge of Impres-
sionist art, Diane mistakenly thinks he's trying to win
her back.
Written by: Ken Levine and David Isaacs
Directed by: James Burrows
Guest Cast: Alison LaPlaca as Paula; Tim Cunningham as
Tim; Al Rosen as the Man Who Said Sinatra
[Note: Nick Colasanto was not in this episode. Sam
shows everyone a photograph Coach sent from Ohio.
It's a smiling Oriental family reunion—the invitation to
the family's relatives went to the wrong address (Coach's
house) and Coach didn't want to disappoint them by
not showing.]

"IF EVER I WOULD (#065) AIR DATE: 2/28/85
LEAVE YOU"
Loretta has left Nick Tortelli and taken him for every-
thing. He comes to Cheers looking for work and hoping
Carla will take him back. She's afraid that she'll be hurt

again, but is almost ready to give in when Loretta comes back and Nick is unable to resist her.
Written by: Ken Levine and David Isaacs
Directed by: James Burrows
Guest Cast: Dan Hedaya as Nick; Jean Kasem as Loretta; Steve Giannelli as Steve
(Note: Coach's absence in this episode is explained as a visit to his sister in Minnesota for a couple of weeks.)

"THE EXECUTIVE'S EXECUTIONER" (#067) AIR DATE: 3/7/85
Norm's boss makes him an offer he can't refuse: accept the job as "Corporate Killer" or be fired himself. Norm devises a unique method of telling people they're fired, but soon his name becomes synonymous with doom and his co-workers avoid any contact with him.
Written by: Heide Perlman
Directed by: James Burrows
Guest Cast: Richard Roat as Mr. Hecht; Larry Harpel as Larry

"BAR BET" (#063) AIR DATE: 3/14/85
An old bet from Sam's drinking past surfaces when Eddie comes into Cheers to remind Sam that if he isn't married to Jacqueline Bisset by midnight tomorrow, he forfeits his bar. Everyone pitches in and they find a sweet young thing with the same name who's willing to marry Sam. Sam backs out knowing it's not fair to her, and Eddie, knowing Sam could have done it, cancels the bet.
Written by: Jim Parker
Directed by: James Burrows
Guest Cast: Michael Richards as Eddie Gordon; Laurie Walters as Jacqueline Bisset; Tom Babson as Tom

"CHEERIO, CHEERS" (#059) AIR DATE: 4/11/85
Frasier will be the visiting scholar at the University of Bologna and asks Diane to come to Europe with him for

191

six months. Diane wants Sam to say anything to convince her to stay, but he doesn't and she goes. She calls from London and it's very obvious they both miss each other very much.

Written by: Sam Simon
Directed by: James Burrows

"THE BARTENDER'S TALE" (#068) AIR DATE: 4/18/85
While Diane is in Europe with Frasier, Sam hires a mature English woman as a waitress. Carla is delighted. The woman is good and there's no chance of romantic entanglements—until her beautiful daughter arrives, and Sam is instantly smitten.

Written by: Sam Simon
Directed by: James Burrows
Guest Cast: Lila Kaye as Lillian; Camilla Moore as Carolyn

"THE BELLES OF ST. CLETE'S" (#069) AIR DATE: 5/2/85
In Europe, Diane and Frasier are beginning to irritate each other; Cliff is getting love letters from a woman he met in Florida on vacation; and Carla could swear her old nemesis from St. Clete's has come into Cheers. None of her old school friends believes it's her—Carla must be mistaken. Carla is out for revenge, and when she finds out the old woman *is* Drusilla, she plans her attack, only to end up liking her.

Written by: Ken Estin
Directed by: James Burrows
Guest Cast: Camila Ashland as Drusilla DiMeglio; Kate Zentall as Kathy; Ellen Gerstein as Mo; Catherine Taolone as Donna; Marsha Warfield as Roxane; Steve Giannelli as Steve; Tim Cunningham as Tim; Tom Babson as Tom; Larry Harpel as Larry; Alan Koss as Alan.

"RESCUE ME"   (#060) AIR DATE: 5/9/85
The season's cliff-hanger has Frasier proposing to Diane, and Diane wanting Sam to confess his feelings for her

and stop the wedding. Unbeknownst to Diane, Sam has boarded a plane to do just that, and she has changed the location of the wedding.
Written by: Ken Estin
Directed by: James Burrows
Guest Cast: Martin Ferrero as the Waiter

Fourth Season: 1985—1986

Starring: Ted Danson, Shelley Long, Rhea Perlman, John Ratzenberger, George Wendt, Woody Harrelson, and Kelsey Grammer

"BIRTH, DEATH, LOVE AND RICE"   (#070) AIR DATE: 9/26/85
Sam, back from Italy, was unable to stop Diane's wedding. It's just as well until Frasier, bordering on insanity, arrives and tells Sam that Diane dumped him at the altar and is now working in a convent. Sam can't let Diane waste away like that. He asks her back to Cheers—as a friend. They both knew the old feelings could return, but Sam's willing to take that chance.
(Note: This episode acknowledges Coach's death, and introduces Woody Boyd, a young farm boy who wants to bartend in a big city and had corresponded with Coach.)
Written by: Heide Perlman
Directed by: James Burrows

"WOODY GOES BELLY UP" (#072) AIR DATE: 10/3/85
Frasier tries to gain Diane's pity by working off his bar tab by sweeping the floor, and the guys have chipped in to bring Woody's girlfriend, Beth, to Boston. It seems Woody and Beth both sublimated their sex drive by eating. Once back together, Woody and she begin putting on weight. Over dinner with Sam and Diane, Sam convinces them to do something about their problem.

Woody and Beth leave to do just that, and Sam and Diane begin eating everything in sight.

Written by: Heide Perlman
Directed by: James Burrows
Guest Cast: Amanda Wyss as Beth Curtis; Al Rosen as the Man Who Said Sinatra

"SOMEDAY MY PRINCE   (#075) AIR DATE: 10/17/85
WILL COME"
A man's cashmere coat left in Cheers arouses Diane's curiosity about its owner. She makes a blind date with him, and when he arrives, he's almost everything she'd expected. Diane learns, to her surprise, that good looks are as important to her as money and position, and has to back out of the new relationship.

Written by: Ron Seeley and Norm Gunzenhauser
Directed by: James Burrows
Guest Cast: Frank Dent as Stuart

"THE GROOM WORE   (#071) AIR DATE: 10/25/85
CLEARASIL"
Carla's son Anthony wants to marry Annie. They're both too young, but Carla is powerless to stop them. She says if they don't see or talk to each other for two weeks and still feel the same, she won't stop them. It looks like the wedding is on until Anthony meets Annie's beautiful sister. Carla breathes a sigh of relief: he's a real Tortelli man after all.

Written by: Peter Casey and David Lee
Directed by: James Burrows
Guest Cast: Timothy Williams as Anthony Tortelli; Mandy Ingber as Annie; John Ingle as Professor Moffat; Sherilyn Fenn as Gabrielle

"DIANE'S NIGHTMARE"   (#078) AIR DATE: 10/31/85
Diane learns that Andy, the waitress murderer, is out on parole. She has a nightmare that he's returned to

194

Cheers to kill her and everyone there. When she wakes, Frasier convinces her it's okay—he's been treating Andy. Andy shows up at Cheers with his new girlfriend, and Diane is shocked at how calm everyone is around him, then realizes the whole thing has been a dream.

Written by: David Lloyd
Directed by: James Burrows
Guest Cast: Derek McGrath as Andy; Nancy Cartwright as Cynthia; Tim Cunningham as Tim

"I'LL GLADLY PAY   (#073) AIR DATE: 11/7/85
YOU TUESDAY"
Diane borrows $500 from Sam to buy a rare first edition Hemingway, then makes no moves to repay him. To prove her good intention, Diane gives Sam the book for safekeeping—and Sam, curious, reads it, then has to hide the fact he dropped it in the bathtub. When a customer offers twice what Diane paid for it, Sam won't let her sell it. Now he owes Diane only another $500 to keep it.

Written by: Cheri Eichen and Bill Steinkellner
Directed by: James Burrows
Guest Cast: William Lanteau as Mr. Sayers

"2 GOOD 2 BE 4 REAL"   (#074) AIR DATE: 11/14/85
Out of desperation, Carla places an ad in the personal section of the paper. When no one answers, Sam and the guys think they're doing her a favor by sending her a letter from "Mitch." Carla falls for it, ignoring a real letter that did come. Sam tells her the truth, and Carla decides to give "Vinnie" a try. He turns out to be okay . . . for a mortician.

Written by: Peter Casey and David Lee
Directed by: James Burrows
Guest Cast: Don Lewis as "Sotto" the Mime; Michael Alaimo as Vinnie

"LOVE THY NEIGHBOR"   (#076) AIR DATE: 11/21/85
Norm thinks his next-door neighbor and Vera are having an affair. Carla's cousin, Santo, a P.I., is hired to check it out. Meanwhile, Sam has gone on Dave Richards' radio show and called Diane his "love bunny," and she forces him to read a prepared on-air apology. Norm's neighbor's wife is now hitting on him, and Norm is about to accept until Santo reports there's no affair. Vera couldn't do it; she loves Norm too much.
Written by: David Angell
Directed by: James Burrows
Guest Cast: Miriam Flynn as Phyllis; Ernie Sabella as Santo

"FROM BEER TO ETERNITY"(#079) AIR DATE: 11/28/85
Sam and the Cheers' team have been losing to the guys from Gary's Tavern. The only sport they haven't tried is bowling, and after the challenge is made, Sam learns they don't even have a decent team for that. Woody was a champion bowler, but won't play, having once maimed someone in a bowling alley. Diane is the one who saves the day—but threatens the guys with their lives if they ever tell anyone she can bowl.
Written by: Peter Casey and David Lee
Directed by: James Burrows
Guest Cast: John Calvin as Gary; Tim Cunningham as Tim; Alan Koss as Alan; Steve Giannelli as Steve

"THE BARSTOOLIE"   (#077) AIR DATE: 12/5/85
Cliff panics when he hears his father who deserted him as a child is coming to Cheers to meet him. His dad is an unexpected surprise—he's just like Cliff. Meanwhile, Diane meets Sam's new date and finds her bright and intelligent. Claudia likes Diane, too, and invites her along on their date. Claudia ultimately dumps Sam, and Cliff learns his dad is on the lam for real estate fraud.
Written by: Andy Cowan and David Williger

Directed by: James Burrows
Guest Cast: Dick O'Neill as Mr. Clavin; Claudia Cron as Claudia

"DON JUAN IS HELL" (#080) AIR DATE: 12/12/85
Sam is flattered when Diane uses him as the subject of her thesis on human sexuality, but becomes hurt when he realizes the "Don Juan Syndrome" means he's really a pathetic character. Diane has to convince him that she exaggerated for the paper, and tries to prove that she and Sam, for instance, have a healthy nonsexual friendship.
Written by: Phoef Sutton
Directed by: James Burrows
Guest Cast: Kenneth Tigar as Dr. Greenspon

"FOOLS AND THEIR (#081) AIR DATE: 12/19/85
MONEY"
Woody has been winning the football pools and asks Sam to make a bet with his bookie to parlay his winnings. When Woody wins on all long shots, Sam has to tell him he never placed the bet. He didn't want to see Woody lose his savings. Woody can't get mad—that was the nicest thing anyone ever did for him.
Written by: Heide Perlman
Directed by: James Burrows
Guest Cast: Al Rosen as the Man Who Said Sinatra

"TAKE MY SHIRT . . . (#086) AIR DATE: 1/9/86
PLEASE?"
While Norm attempts to wine and dine two prospective clients in the dairy business, Sam watches hopelessly as his lucky #16 shirt sits on a celebrity auction table with no one bidding. Diane takes pity on him, buys it, and he forces her to return it. Then Sam bids on it himself, and has to return it. Finally someone actually buys it only to return it to Sam. He felt sorry for Sam.

197

Written by: David Lloyd
Directed by: James Burrows
Guest Cast: Robert Symonds as Mr. Brubaker; Frances Bay as Mrs. Brubaker; Earl Bullock as the Announcer; Patrick Cronin as Bert

"SUSPICION"   (#082) AIR DATE: 1/16/86
Diane's class experiment in group paranoia results in everyone at Cheers vowing to get even. When a local TV crew shows up to film Boston's new poets, Diane knows this is it. She does an embarrassing rendition of a chicken only to learn the TV show was for real. Upset they hadn't even tried to get even, she goes into Sam's office. When a bucketful of water lands on her, she knows she's loved and accepted.
Written by: Tom Reeder
Directed by: James Burrows

"THE TRIANGLE"   (#083) AIR DATE: 1/23/86
Frasier's still in the dumps and Diane feels if he can cure someone he'll snap out of it. She gets Sam to pretend he's having problems with his sex life. Frasier feels it's because he still loves Diane. Sam and Diane are forced to admit they still love each other, and another fight ensues. Frasier isn't a happy man, but at least he's in better condition than they are.
Written by: Susan Segar
Directed by: James Burrows

"CLIFFY'S BIG SCORE"   (#085) AIR DATE: 1/30/86
Cliff is in big trouble—both Diane and Carla have accepted his invitation to the Postmen's Award Banquet. He manages to fix Carla up with a friend, and at Carla's suggestion, Cliff puts the make on Diane after "running out of gas" on a lonely road. Diane quickly makes him see the error of his ways and leaves him in the dust.
Written by: Heide Perlman

198

Directed by: James Burrows
Guest Cast: Kathleen Freeman as Coreen; Al Rosen as the Man Who Said Sinatra

"SECOND TIME AROUND" (#084) AIR DATE: 2/6/86
Sam decides to fix Frasier up with Candi (with an "i"—like Gandhi). Frasier resents it until he meets her and falls for her. They almost get married until Diane makes him see that the differences between them will keep the marriage from working.
Written by: Cheri Eichen and Bill Steinkellner
Directed by: Tom Lofaro
Guest Cast: Jennifer Tilly as Candi Pearson; Bebe Neuwirth as Dr. Lillith Sternin

"THE PETERSON PRINCIPLE" (#087) AIR DATE: 2/13/86
Norm is up against one other man for a big promotion. He learns his competition is sleeping with the boss's wife, but never says anything, hoping to win on his own merits. He ultimately loses because Vera didn't fit in with the other wives, but Norm tells her it was his own fault they passed him by.
Written by: Peter Casey and David Lee
Directed by: James Burrows
Guest Cast: Chip Zien as Jeff Robbins; Daniel Davis as Mr. Reinhardt

"DARK IMAGININGS" (#088) AIR DATE: 2/20/86
Sam, trying to prove he's still young, gives himself a hernia playing racquetball with Woody. Diane, Carla, and Woody all stop by to cheer him up as he lies in the hospital with an "old man's illness," feeling his life is over.
Written by: David Angell
Directed by: James Burrows
Guest Cast: Pamela Bach as Bonnie

"SAVE THE LAST DANCE FOR ME" (#089) AIR DATE: 2/27/86

Carla and Nick team up for the Boston Boppers' dance contest, but after several fights, Nick decides to take Loretta, and Carla asks Sam to be her partner. Neither pair is winning, and finally Nick tells the judges he'll show them how it should look, and reteams with Carla to win the contest.
Written by: Heide Perlman
Directed by: James Burrows
Guest Cast: Dan Hedaya as Nick Tortelli; Jean Kasem as Loretta

"FEAR IS MY CO-PILOT" (#090) AIR DATE: 3/13/86

Jack, an adventurer/pilot friend of Diane's, offers to take her and Sam for a ride in his small plane, and in mid-flight suddenly collapses, leaving Sam and Diane to ponder their fate. They both admit they wish things had turned out differently. In the midst of their confession, Jack reappears. He was faking—he just wanted them to really "taste life."
Written by: Cheri Eichen and Bill Steinkellner
Directed by: James Burrows
Guest Cast: Joseph Whipp as Jack Dalton

"DIANE CHAMBERS DAY" (#091) AIR DATE: 3/20/86

Diane feels very left out when the whole gang goes to Sam's to watch *The Magnificent Seven* on TV and she isn't invited. They try to make it up to her by taking her to the opera. Diane is very impressed at Sam's choice, while Frasier fumes. It was all *his* idea.
Written by: Kimberly Hill
Directed by: James Burrows
Guest Cast: Doris Grau as Corinne; Al Rosen as the Man Who Said Sinatra

"RELIEF BARTENDER"   (#095) AIR DATE: 3/27/86
Competition from other sports figures owning bars in
the area convinces Sam to become a manager/host and
hire a second bartender, Ken. Sam is a terrible host, but
the new bartender is making a lot of new friends. Sam
decides to return to working the bar and has to let one
of the bartenders go . . . Woody. When Sam learns Ken
has been offered a better job, he has to try to win
Woody back.
Written by: Miriam Trogdon
Directed by: James Burrows
Guest cast: Tony Carreiro as Ken

"STRANGE BEDFELLOWS—   (#092) AIR DATE: 5/1/86
PART I"
A beautiful councilwoman stops by Cheers on a hand-
shake tour of the city, and Sam is instantly smitten. She
also is drawn to Sam and a serious romance develops.
Diane is sure her motives are just to win votes by being
seen with Sam. Diane and Frasier, who wants to be near
Diane, go to work for the competition, and watch helplessly as Janet wins and kisses Sam in front of all the TV
cameras.

"STRANGE BEDFELLOWS—   (#093) AIR DATE: 5/8/86
PART II"
Senator Gary Hart makes a cameo appearance. Janet
wants Sam to fire Diane. She's just insecure enough not
to want an old girlfriend still around, and Sam finally
agrees it isn't good for Diane to still be there. She
should get her own life started. Diane overhears their
conversation and tries to resign before Sam can fire her.

"STRANGE BEDFELLOWS— (#094) AIR DATE: 5/15/86
PART III"
Diane overhears Janet asking Sam for a commitment,
and at the press conference following, she poses as a

reporter and asks Sam his intentions regarding the councilwoman. Sam humiliates himself trying to get Diane to shut up, and ends up losing Diane and Janet, who feels he doesn't respect her or her position. Alone, and knowing his life is a mess, Sam picks up the phone. He asks the woman who answers to marry him.

Written by: David Angell
Directed by: James Burrows
Guest Cast: Kate Mulgrew as Janet Eldridge; Max Wright as Jim Fleener; David Paymer as Phil Schumacher; Alan Koss as Alan; Tim Cunningham as Tim; Steve Giannelli as Steve

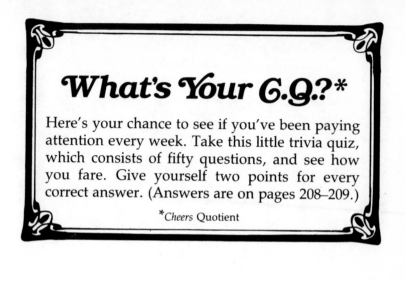

What's Your C.Q.?*

Here's your chance to see if you've been paying attention every week. Take this little trivia quiz, which consists of fifty questions, and see how you fare. Give yourself two points for every correct answer. (Answers are on pages 208–209.)

*Cheers Quotient

TRUE OR FALSE?

1. Sam Malone never finished high school.
2. Diane attended Radcliffe.
3. Diane's nickname is Muffin.
4. Carla's wedding reception was held in a bowling alley.
5. Norm drives a Honda Civic.
6. Woody bowls every chance he gets.
7. Norm has never been unfaithful.
8. Cliff was once married to a woman who later entered a convent.
9. Norm worked for Sam.
10. Sam is a confirmed bachelor and has never been married.

TAKE YOUR PICK (Multiple choice)

1. Sam Malone's brother is . . .
   a. Mark
   b. Lawrence
   c. Derek
   d. Cameron

2. Diane Chambers once admitted herself to what sanitarium?
   a. Golden Brook
   b. Happy Acres
   c. Pleasanton
   d. Carefree Haven
3. What branch of the armed forces did Coach join?
   a. Army
   b. Air Force
   c. Marines
   d. Navy
4. The Chambers' family chauffeur's name is . . .
   a. Boggs
   b. Sherman
   c. Arnold
   d. Watson
5. The Coach's daughter's name is . . .
   a. Sally
   b. Nancy
   c. Lisa
   d. Sherry

WHO, WHAT, WHEN, WHERE . . .

1. Who is Truman?
2. What does Frasier Crane's mother do for a living?
3. Where were Diane and Sumner supposed to go on their honeymoon?
4. How did Carla acquire her talent for repairing things?
5. Did Sam Malone buy the bar before or after quitting baseball?
6. Who was proud of the fact that he was on the high school audiovisual squad?
7. Who considers Chicken McNuggets his/her favorite food?
8. Where did Diane's parents meet?
9. Who once worked in the kitchen of a convent?
10. How did Norm get his nickname Moonglow?

11. Who or what was Smiley?
12. What is Norm's profession?
13. Who is Beth Curtis?
14. Who has a brother who's a lawyer?
15. Name Diane's deceased cat.

FILL ME IN . . .
1. _____ drives a Studebaker.
2. Mr. Jammers is Diane's stuffed _____.
3. Coach played _____ for the St. Louis Browns.
4. Sam's good-luck charm is a _____.
5. Diane dumped her first true love because he returned from boot camp with _____.
6. Pavlov is the name of _____'s dog.
7. _____ graduated from Dean Acheson High School.
8. Woody hails from the state of _____.
9. Diane met Sumner while _____.
10. "Red" was _____'s nickname.

NUMBERS GAME
1. How many years was Coach married?
2. In what year was Cheers established, according to the sign over the entrance?
3. What year did Sam buy Cheers?
4. After leaving Frasier Crane, how many months did Diane spend in Europe?
5. How many children did Carla have with Nick?
6. Who graduated thirtieth in his high-school class?
7. How many years after buying Cheers did Sam join Alcoholics Anonymous?
8. What was the number of Sam's Red Sox uniform?
9. What was Sam's highest batting average?
10. The year that Cliff was voted Postman of the Year, how many other mailmen received the same honor?

207

ANSWERS:

TRUE OR FALSE?

1. True
2. False; Boston University
3. False; Carla's nickname is Muffin
4. True
5. True
6. False; after a bizarre accident during a game of bowling, Woody vowed never to bowl again
7. True
8. False; Cliff was never married
9. True
10. False; he was married briefly to a woman named Deborah

TAKE YOUR PICK

1. c
2. a
3. d
4. a
5. c

WHO, WHAT, WHEN, WHERE . . .

1. Woody's dog
2. She's a psychiatrist
3. Barbados
4. Her ex-husband was handy and she picked up his talent
5. Before
6. Norm Peterson
7. Carla
8. In Europe during the war
9. Diane
10. During a high-school wrestling match, his opponent pulled down Norm's gym shorts
11. Coach's boyhood dog
12. Accountant

13. Woody's girlfriend back home
14. Sam Malone
15. Elizabeth Barrett Browning

FILL ME IN

1. Cliff
2. Giraffe
3. Catcher
4. Bottle cap from last beer he consumed
5. A terrible haircut
6. Frasier Crane
7. Norm Peterson
8. Indiana
9. Attending college
10. Coach

NUMBERS GAME

1. Thirty
2. 1895
3. 1976
4. Six
5. Five
6. Norm
7. Three
8. Sixteen
9. .149
10. 266

Plume

THE TALK OF THE TOWN . . .

(0452)

☐ **HOLLYWOOD BABYLON II, by Kenneth Anger.** You'll just devour this feast of revelations that features names like Audrey Hepburn, Truman Capote, Elizabeth Taylor, Doris Day, Judy Garland, Frank Sinatra, Clark Gable, John Wayne, and so many more names whose faces you know so well, but whose secrets are now revealed in a way that you never imagined outside your wildest and most wicked fantasies. . . .   (257212—$12.95)

☐ **THE COTTON CLUB, by Jim Haskins.** It was the showplace of legendary entertainers like Ella Fitzgerald, Louis Armstrong, and Cab Calloway . . . it was the property of some of the roughest mobsters in Manhattan . . . it was the favorite haunt of everybody who was anybody—Ethel Merman, Irving Berlin, Fred Astaire, Florenz Ziegfeld, and so many others. Now, in vibrant words and vivid pictures, are the times, the people, and the magic of the Cotton Club.   (255988—$9.95)

☐ **MOVIE COMEDY TEAMS, by Leonard Maltin.** From Laurel and Hardy, to the three Stooges, to Abbott and Costello, here are the inside stories of Hollywood's unforgettable comedians. Writer-critic Maltin reveals their private sorrows and public triumphs, and colorfully details the high—and low—points of their careers.   (256941—$9.95)

☐ **AMERICAN FILM NOW: The People, The Power, The Money, The Movies by James Monaco.** Revised edition. Hollywood movies today are bigger—but are they better than ever? In this major examination of modern American cinema, one of our leading film critics ponders this question in a sweeping study of Hollywood today.   (255457—$14.95)

All prices higher in Canada.

Meridian

(0452)

DEO MOVIEMAKERS HANDBOOK by Frank Ledlie Moore. This indispensable reference work and how-to manual offers all the know-how you need to take full advantage of this new world of creative opportunity. It describes the latest equipment and accessories and details what they can do, and makes suggestions for different kinds of video films, including home movies, dramatic productions, commercials, and much, much more. (256127—$12.95)

☐ **THE SONGWRITER'S RHYMING DICTIONARY by Sammy Cahn.** Contains more than 50,000 rhyme words—arranged in terms of sounds and syllables—for writers of songs, jingles, and light verse, by the great Academy Award-winning lyricist, plus Sammy's memorable anecdotes about his collaboration with the likes of Bing Crosby, Frank Sinatra, and others. There is no better guide if you have a song in your heart but trouble finding the words. (006783—$8.95)

☐ **THE BASIC BOOK OF PHOTOGRAPHY by Tom Grimm.** Newly revised and updated. With a superbly lucid text and many invaluable illustrations, covering all aspects of photography from selecting the camera that's right for you to mounting your finished photos, this long-needed guide belongs on every photographer's shelf. (257484—$8.95)

☐ **MAGIC WRITING: A Writer's Guide to Word Processing by John Stratton with Dorothy Stratton.** If you are a writer thinking about switching to a word processor, this complete guide will tell you in words you will understand how to choose, master, and benefit from a word processor. Plus a computerese-English dictionary and glossary. (255635—$12.95)

Prices slightly higher in Canada.

To order use coupon on next page.